ROBERT BRUCE

" By far the most finished figure among all the makers of
Scotland."

Dr. Alexander Whyte.

ROBERT BRUCE

MINISTER IN THE KIRK OF EDINBURGH

By

D. C. MACNICOL, B.D.

" Not with enticing words of man's wisdom, but in demonstration
of the Spirit and of power." 1 Cor. ii. 4.

THE BANNER OF TRUTH TRUST
1961

First published 1907, Oliphant, Anderson and Ferrier.
Reprinted 1961, Banner of Truth Trust.

Originally dedicated: "To My Wife."

This book is set in 10-point Bookprint and
printed and bound in Great Britain by
Billing and Sons Limited, Guildford and
London

CONTENTS

CONTENTS

INTRODUCTION

It was the glory of the theology of the Reformation that for the first time in the history of the Church the doctrine of the Holy Spirit was fully developed. John Calvin, as B. B. Warfield has shown, was pre-eminently the theologian of the Holy Spirit, and it is not surprising that in the period following the Reformation, when this theology was most firmly implanted in our land, there arose a school of preachers through whom the Spirit worked in such almighty power that it resulted in one of the profoundest spiritual movements in our national history. There have indeed been several periods in Church history when Britain has been shaken by men preaching " in demonstration of the Spirit and of power," yet it can hardly be questioned that no century has witnessed such a succession of Spirit-filled men as the years 1560-1660.[1] Edward Deering, William Perkins, Henry Smith, Samuel Fairclough, John Rogers, Samuel Ward, John Preston, Stephen Marshall, are but a few of the names that spring to mind in England, and Scotland, as this book will show, was no less favoured.

John Knox died in 1572, bequeathing to his successors an example of prophetic preaching which they were not likely to forget. The sixty years following that date provide the background of this narrative and the man who was then one of the most commanding figures in Scotland is the subject.

Amidst the paucity of biographical information that has been handed down from the seventeenth century it is some consolation that there were at least enough materials for the author to write in 1907 a life of *Master Robert Bruce*. For Bruce typifies many of the best qualities of the old Scottish and Puri-

---

[1] The closest parallel is probably to be seen in Wales, 1740-1840, and the Welsh preachers of that time, both in their theology and preaching, closely resemble the best preachers of this period.

tan divines. The light of the presence of the Spirit of God—the characteristic of his school—can be seen throughout his minis-try. If men want to know how evangelicals lived and preached three hundred and fifty years ago they can do no better than to study Robert Bruce.

As the young minister of St. Giles, Edinburgh, we read in Wodrow of "the extraordinary effusion of the Spirit when he first dispensed the Sacrament of the Supper";[1] and Fleming tells us how "the power and efficacy of the Spirit most sensibly accompanying the word he preached" made his ministry "as a great light through the whole land."[2] Years later we still find Bruce praying, "May it please the Lord to triple His Spirit upon me";[3] banished to the north the same Divine presence overflowed his soul—"I am the happiest man that ever was born"[4]—and as an old man, close to the end, he can write to a friend, "I never got such access in my time as I have gotten since I went from you . . . His Spirit has testified to my spirit, not only by real joys, spiritual and elevated light, but by vocal speeches within me in the daylight, that I heard so sensibly with great effusion of tears."[5] Truly Robert Bruce could say with the Apostle Paul, "Our sufficiency is of God; who also hath made us able ministers of the new testament; not of the letter, but of the Spirit."[6] It is not surprising that we read of such a man counselling a vain young preacher in these telling words: "I found your sermon very polished and digested, but there is one thing I miss in it—*the Spirit of God*."[7]

It will be noticed in this book how the abundant measure of the Spirit which Bruce and his fellows received was not without the earnest use of means. "Nothing is won without great dili-gence," was their principle. The Word of God was constantly in their hands (as an old man Bruce could testify that "he is not within the Isle of Britain of my age that takes greater pains upon his Bible") and, supremely, they were men of prayer. The old description of Bruce by Robert Fleming has never been

---

[1] Wodrow's *Life of Bruce*, p. 145.   [2] *Ibid.*, p. 143.
[3] *Ibid.*, p. 191.   [4] *Ibid.*, p. 223.   [5] *Ibid.*, p. 251.
[6] 2 Cor. iii. 5-6.   [7] Wodrow's *Life of Bruce*, p. 234.

bettered: " Mr. Bruce was a great wrestler who had more than ordinary familiarity with his Master. He was very short in prayer when others were present; but every sentence was like a strong bolt shot up to heaven. I have heard him say that he wearied when others were long in prayer, but being alone, he spent much time in wrestling and prayer."[1]

This aspect of Bruce's character will appear in the following pages, but as there is one eminent instance of his power in prayer which the author has omitted to narrate we will, for the sake of completeness, record it here. The event is reported by Fleming who received it from the daughter of the home in which it took place:

" A little before his death, Mr. Bruce was at Edinburgh, and at this time, through his age and weakness, he was obliged to keep his chamber. At that time there was a meeting of godly serious ministers at Edinburgh, upon the accounts they had got of the innovations the Bishops were about to bring in upon this Church, particularly their design of introducing the Common Prayer Book. When they knew of Mr. Bruce's being in town, a good many of them came to his chamber, and communicated to him the accounts they had of the prelates' designs, and their own procedure. After some conversation, Mr. Bruce at their desire prayed, and in his prayer he laid before the Lord the substance of what they had been representing, which, in short, was the present lamentable state of the Church; and this he did with such extraordinary motion upon the hearts of all present, and so sensible an out-pouring of the Spirit, as scarce any present were able to contain themselves; and, which was much more extraordinary, there were several persons in the other rooms of the house, who, till afterwards, did not know that in Mr. Bruce's room they were at prayer, who, at that instant, felt an unusual motion, and seriousness upon their minds, though they knew not the cause of it. That great and learned man, and ornament of his country, Mr. John Wemyss of Lathocker, was occasionally present at that meeting with Mr. Bruce, and when he came out, said, " O! what a strange man is

[1] Wodrow's *Life of Bruce*, pp. 142 and 144.

this, for he knocked down the Spirit of God upon us all," alluding to a motion Mr. Bruce used with his hands upon the table at which he stood."[1]

"If ye call on the Father, who without respect of persons judgeth according to every man's work, pass the time of your sojourning here in fear: Forasmuch as ye know that ye were . . . redeemed . . . with the precious blood of Christ."[2] In the spirit of this apostolic injunction Robert Bruce passed his earthly pilgrimage. He feared dishonouring God,[3] he feared offending his Saviour—" Let not my union to my Lord Jesus be impaired "[4]—and he feared that trouble of conscience which is consequent upon grieving the Holy Spirit—" Let my conscience be without hurt. *The burning of the carcass in a hot lead* is nothing to the trouble of conscience."[5] This is not the place to show how Bruce's sense of God was born of that vision of the Divine glory which lies at the heart of Reformed theology. It is no accident that Calvinism, which is evangelicalism in its purity, has moulded the strongest and boldest men that ever stood in a pulpit; men who feared not the faces of man; men whose very blood was as iron. Such are the men that Britain needs today. May God arise and send them forth!

The Publishers.

August, 1960.

[1] Wodrow's *Life of Bruce*, pp. 151-152.   [2] 1 Pet. i. 17-19.
[3] Wodrow's *Life of Bruce*, cf. the remarkable story on p. 211.
[4] *Ibid.*, p. 176.   [5] *Ibid.*, pp. 177 and 292.

CHAPTER I

Kinsfolk and Connections of Robert Bruce

THERE may be seen to-day in the kirkyard of Larbert, not very far distant from the tower of the modern church, a grave which gathers about it still the profound devotion of Scottish people, though nearly three hundred years have rolled by since it was digged. This historic sepulchre, while it is near to the western end of the modern Parish Church, is actually within the precincts of the pre-Reformation church which stood till the year 1820 in the kirkyard of Larbert. Master Robert Bruce, laird of Kinnaird and minister of Edinburgh, is the man whose dust rests in this holy ground. His piety restored the church, which had been neglected and deserted before the Reformation; his preaching gave distinction to the pulpit at the foot of which his mortal remains were laid in the year 1631.

A flat gravestone covers the spot. And here is the inscription upon it—the epitaph carved upon Bruce's tomb by the men of his own time. In the centre is the coat of arms of that distinguished Stirlingshire house from which Robert Bruce was sprung, a saltier in chief, a mullet in dexter side. The initials R.B. slightly defaced by a huge crack in the stone, the date at the top, 1631, with M beneath for the " Master," are easily deciphered, and these words in Latin, *Cristus in vita et in morte lucrum.*[1]

The Scotsman whose grave is beneath that old stone was one of the great Reformation leaders. His career bridges the interval between Knox and Melville on the one side, and Alexander Henderson on the other. Of Knox he could have said *Virgilium vidi tantum*; Melville was his master who gave its impetus to

[1] " Christ is to me both in life and in death advantage."

II

his resolute career; Henderson was his most famous disciple—the leader of the second Reformation.

The place occupied by Robert Bruce among his contemporaries was unique. Called early to the greatest pulpit in Scotland, that of Knox himself, he became at once the voice of the Church. So strong and so sustained was his power that, whether encountering royal favour or persecution, his ministry was sought after with an undiminished and even an increasing fervour throughout a long generation of time. His antagonists spoke of his bewitching the people, but on the other hand there is a unanimous testimony from his contemporaries of the Scottish Church Party, and especially from his brethren of the ministry, as to the exceptional and splendid position in which Bruce's gifts and his sanctity enshrined him. " That confessor, almost martyr of the Lord Jesus," are the words of Andrew Melville, his teacher. " No man since the apostles' time spake with such power," said a disciple of Bruce, John Livingstone, with enthusiasm. " Bruce," cried the Church historian Calderwood, " may my soul at the last be with thine."

While there is no certainty about the date or the place of Robert Bruce's birth, it is probable that he was born at Airth Castle in Stirlingshire in the year 1554. There is nothing recorded of his boyhood, and not till that moment when young men are confronted with grave problems of personal decision does he step into our view. It is told by himself, in that frank narrative written in his old age of which only a few fragments have been preserved, that about the period of his passing out of boyhood, deep, anxious reflections concerning sin and the way of salvation haunted his mind. As early as the year 1571, when he was about seventeen years of age, and when he was at the point of taking his degree at St. Andrews University, he tells that he could not mount on horseback nor alight without an accusing conscience.[1] The thoughts of his heart troubled him day and night. Here, surely, was a sore situation for a young student. But perhaps there are more lads in their later teens suffering from stress of conscience than the world is aware of. Young

[1] Calderwood's *History of the Kirk*, iv. p. 635.

Bruce had little help in his home: his mother was a bigoted Catholic; and the old laird was engrossed, it appears, with other concerns. For at least ten years, as a student of arts and of law, the young man carried his burden solitary, like Christian on his way to the Interpreter's House. One marked result was a precocity, a gravity of demeanour, which struck all observers. And no doubt it was the possession of these qualities, as well as the influence of his rank, that led to Bruce being thrust early into positions of responsibility in the Church.

The claim of this family of Airth to high rank in Scotland could be established both on the male and on the female side. Indeed, they could trace the nearest descent of any of their name to the blood royal.[1] Sir Alexander Bruce, the laird of Airth, could show a direct descent from King Robert the Bruce; while his wife, Janet Livingstone, had a genealogy no less eminent, being a great-granddaughter of James I and of Jane Beaufort his Queen. A sister of this Janet Livingstone was Mary Livingstone, one of the " four Marys " who were maids of honour to Mary, Queen of Scots. Sempill, of Beltrees, married Mary Livingstone, and their son, a cousin of Robert Bruce, the minister, used his influence with the king more than once in after days on behalf of his persecuted relative.[2]

The family of Airth was not only high born; it had some claim also to distinction in the public service. The grandfather of our Reformer is famous in history for his spirited defence of Edinburgh Castle against an invading English army. A Sir John Bruce, of Airth, was in 1481 charged by the commissioners to call Alexander, Duke of Albany, to answer for the charge of treason. Sir Alexander, the father of Master Robert Bruce, was a rude, bluff baron, with a goodly proportion of acres for his estate, and behind him a powerful following of retainers. On one occasion, supported by his trusty followers, he encountered a party of the retainers of the laird of Weems in the High Street of Edinburgh, whom he attacked and pistolled, the skirmish being a very bloody one.[3] He was credited

[1] Hill Burton, *History of Scotland*, vol. v. p. 340.
[2] See pp. 129-130.　　　　[3] Birrel's *Diary*, p. 13.

too, in company with his kinsman and neighbour, the laird of Dunipace, with having prompted the slaughter in 1595 of David Forrester, a Stirling man, who was in the service of Lord Mar. This deed was reckoned one of the most foul in that troubled period; and the earl, to express his abhorrence of the crime, adopted a dramatic fashion of interring the corpse of Forrester. In front of the funeral procession he caused to be borne a white sheet upon which had been rudely depicted a portrait of the dead man, with the bloody wounds upon it. In this wise, with every token of defiance of the murderers and honour to the dead, the funeral cortège passed close by the very residence of Bruce to the place of burial at Stirling.[1]

A better side of Alexander Bruce's energetic character is shown in the generosity with which he dealt towards brothers, nephews, and dependants. He was lavish to a fault, and his descendants judged him too liberal with his possessions, even to the impoverishing of his estate.[2]

The family of Janet Livingstone, mother of Robert Bruce, like that of his father, had borne itself well in the service of the kingdom. Alexander, fifth Lord Livingstone, the grandfather, had a reputation for great integrity, so that into his hands the education of Mary, Queen of Scots, was committed, a responsibility which he discharged with faithfulness. The Livingstone family were Roman Catholic, and they were strongly opposed to the Reformation. The children of Sir Alexander Bruce and Dame Janet Livingstone were seven in number, two daughters and five sons. William, the eldest son, died during the lifetime of his father, leaving a son who became heir in entail. The second son was Master Robert, scholar and Presbyterian minister. The third son, Sir John, who had Kincavel and Westborland in Denny for his inheritance, was a man of fine character. We shall meet him more than once, standing side by side with

---

[1] Spottiswood, *History*, p. 411. The Bruce who was an accomplice in this deed was the eldest son of Alexander "Bruce younger of Airth."—Pitcairn, *Criminal Trials*, i. 351.

[2] For the details of the Bruce family history recorded in this chapter the author is indebted to M. E. Cumming Bruce's *Family Records of the Bruces and the Cumyns* (Blackwood, 1870), pp. 350-372.

his distinguished brother, Robert, a support to him in his troubled career. Sir Alexander Bruce, of Bangour in Ireland, was the fourth son, while curiously enough the fifth son, like the second, was called Robert. It was not uncommon at the period to find a Christian name recur in the same family. In the family archives this Robert junior (as he is styled) is described as brother-german; and while the more illustrious Robert threw in his lot with the Reformers, the other appears to have adhered to the Roman Catholic faith. He was a priest, and had from his father " the chaplanrie of our Ladie aisle, founded and situated on the south side of the Kirk of Airth."

Everywhere in the neighbourhood of Airth are to be found signs that the Bruce family were once in possession of the land. The village cross, still to be seen in the main street of Airth, bears upon one side of it the ancient Bruce arms, on the other the arms of the Elphinstone family with the motto " Do well, let them say," the initials C.E. (Charles Elphinstone). In the chapel adjoining the castle, and on the gravestones which are huddled around it, one can decipher the names or the insignia of countless generations of Bruces, those knights and dames who of old dwelt here and had their being, and whose laughter filled those corridors with life. Today their dust fills the crowded kirkyard. There is one stone bearing the arms of Bruce of Airth, and the letters A.B., which is declared on good authority to be undoubtedly the coat of arms of Sir Alexander Bruce (died 1600), father of Master Robert Bruce, the Reformer.

The ancient Castle of Airth, standing upon its abrupt rock high above the carse, is a composite pile, the oldest portion dating back to the twelfth century. Once upon a time the tide washed the castle rock, though to-day the river bank is nearly a mile distant. A portion of the castle is traditionally linked on to the days of Sir William Wallace. In " Blind Harry " it is related that an uncle of Wallace, priest in the parish of Duni- pace, had been caught by English soldiers, and thrown into a dark dungeon which lay beneath the castle. Wallace of course attacked and slew the garrison, releasing their prisoner. To this day there is shown a Wallace tower in the western wing of the castle, a portion of which authorities declare belongs to the latter part of the twelfth century.

There is in the Castle of Airth a Wallace room with ancient oaken wainscoting, which claims the attention of every patriotic visitor. But there is another chamber in an adjoining, newer wing of the building, which has at present a stronger claim upon our attention. There is no sure tradition indicating the exact room which Robert Bruce in his narrative describes as the " New Loft Chamber." In was in this room that, three hundred years after Wallace fought his fight, the young Scottish student, Bruce, encountered a struggle big with consequences both to his own career and to the Church of his native land. The great battles of history have been fought in the intellect and the heart. It was a struggle of this kind which went on within the soul of Bruce on a summer night of the year 1581, as he lay in the New Loft Chamber of his father's castle. There is an inscription shown to this day upon the wall of one of the vaults upon which the castle stands, " Let tham say, 1581." It is strange that this was the very year of Robert Bruce's memorable conflict and decision. The sculptured motto upon yonder wall may be regarded as his testimony, on the night when, defiant of training and tradition, he cut his way through every barrier, and was obedient to the heavenly voice. Many tides of invasion have beaten against the rock of Airth; the most insidious of them all, threatening to sap the independence of the Scottish Church and to replace the fetters of Rome, was that tide of alien Episcopacy against the inroads of which Robert Bruce from the first to the last of a long career opposed himself. What he stood for was in its essence freedom of conscience and the liberties of the people; and it must be the verdict of history that he did not make his stand in vain. Vanished from the earth are all those bright dames and bold knights who once on a time occupied so proud a place in the activities of this realm; yet unquenched to the present hour in its essentials is the contention of our stout-hearted Reformer. We have entered into possession of that spiritual freedom which he and his comrades suffered to secure. Such men as these are the shadow of a great rock in a weary land, into the shelter of which many creep as to their hiding-place. They are knots upon the thread of a nation's progress. They have laboured, and we are entered into their labours.

CHAPTER II

The Last Night of August, the Year of God 1581

THERE are conspicuous dates in the career of Robert Bruce round which his story revolves. These are marked carefully in the narrative written by himself. And it is worthy of note that if the year of Bruce's birth is uncertain, he leaves us in no doubt as to the exact time of his conversion. This is given with much circumstance in his own story of the last night of August, 1581.

The parents of Bruce had marked out for their clever son a career widely different from that of a minister of the Gospel. His mother, belonging as she did to the haughty Catholic family of Livingstone, was specially averse to giving her consent. Neither she, however, nor his kind father grudged him the best education in their power. Their eldest son, as befitted the heir, was educated at home; while the second son, Robert, after a course of philosophy at St. Andrews, was sent abroad to continue his studies in those lands to which in the sixteenth century the best scholarship of Europe was still confined.

The date of Bruce's enrolment as a student at St. Andrews can be ascertained with exactitude, and the name of the college which he attended. James Melville entered St. Leonard's in the year 1569[1] at the age of thirteen, and Bruce, being just a year or two Melville's senior, must have begun his curriculum about the same date. The University Records give the name Robertus Brus among students incorporated from St. Salvator's College in the year 1568. The name occurs twice thereafter, amongst the Bachelors of 1571 and amongst the Masters of Arts

---

[1] James Melville curiously gives the wrong date in his *Diary*. The Records of St. Andrews University give 1569. See Brown's *Knox*, vol. ii. p. 267.

of 1572.[1] These dates correspond with other information which we possess, and they cast much light upon the career of Bruce. If, as is probable, he was born in 1554, then he was exactly fourteen when he came up to college, which is the same age as Andrew Melville had attained when he entered St. Mary's.

It is not difficult to assign a reason why Bruce's parents chose St. Salvator's and not St. Leonard's or St. Mary's as the college for their son. St. Salvator's, commonly known as "The Auld College," was of the three colleges that one which still adhered to the elder faith. There was what worthy Richard Bannatyne calls a "privie hatred" cherished at St. Andrews against St. Leonard's. The latter was the very home of the Reformation, so that it was commonly said of those who imbibed the new teaching that they had "drunk of St. Leonard's Well." George Buchanan held the principalship of St. Leonard's from 1566 to 1570, and his fame led to that college being crowded with students at the expense of the rival colleges. The numbers who attended the university were at no time large as compared with continental universities. For example, in the year 1569, when James Melville entered St. Andrews for the first time, the whole number of fresh entrants was but forty-three.[2]

More important in the direction of Bruce's career than any other influence was the personality of the veteran Knox himself. By comparing the dates we discover the significant fact that Knox's last year of residence at St. Andrews coincided with a part of Bruce's undergraduate course. Coming to the city in July 1571, he remained till August 1572, preaching every Sunday and teaching the Prophet Daniel, "always applying his text (as a faithful preacher ought to do) according to the time and state of the people."[3] Like James Melville, who from his college of St. Leonard's attended these weekly sermons, and was profoundly influenced by the preacher, Bruce would of

---

[1] Mr. J. Maitland Anderson, the librarian of St. Andrews University, kindly made a search of which the above is the result. He adds: "There is nothing by which he can be identified, but I suppose there need be no doubt about the man."

[2] Hume Brown's *George Buchanan*, pp. 227-242.

[3] Richard Bannatyne, quoted Laing's *Knox*, vol. vi. p. 624.

course be drawn inevitably to hear John Knox. We do not know whether the friendship between Melville and Bruce, afterwards so intimate, was begun when together they sat at the feet of Knox. Surely the following immortal picture drawn by the former must be taken to include in it Bruce also: " Master Knox would sometimes come in and repose him in our college yard, and call us scholars to him, and bless us, and exhort us to know God and His work in our country, and stand by the good cause; to use our time well, and learn the good instructions, and follow the good example of our masters." Or, if the feuds of the rival colleges would prevent such close intercourse, we must at least believe that both the youths would hear Knox, as he discoursed from the pulpit with an effect which the Diarist Melville describes: " I had my pen and my little book, and took away such things as I could comprehend. In the opening up of his text he was moderate in the space of an half hour; but when he entered to application he made me so to grew and tremble that I could not hold a pen to write."[1]

Knox soon after left St. Andrews, returning to Edinburgh to die. Yet he had not lived his last year among the students in vain. What a picture it is! The old man, like a Hebrew prophet, bending over the lads with whom lay the future; looking into their faces with wistful desire to find out what might be in them; praying over them, that they might partake in the grace of God, and be good servants of their country. The voice of Knox, " which was able to put more life into us than six hundred trumpets continually blustering in our ears," roused the conscience of one and another of the students; the spell of the Reformation and the spirit of the living Christ thereafter directed their careers.

The regular curriculum at St. Andrews extended to four years. In the conferring of degrees a certain favour was shown to persons of rank, amongst whom Robert Bruce would, of course, be classified. On general grounds, however, of scholarship Bruce would be fully qualified for his degree, and in 1572, the very year of Knox's death, he attained to his mastership,

---

[1] James Melville's *Diary*, p. 26.

being solemnly laureated by the Chancellor, *Master* Robert Bruce, " in nomine Patris, Filii, et Spiritus Sancti." The title Master, which was thereafter prefixed to Bruce's name, being used regularly both by his fellow-citizens and his fellow-Presbyterians in addressing him, is an academic and not a clerical prefix. It was in great favour during mediæval times, being the token of a degree, Master of Arts, which qualified to lecture and teach in the seven liberal arts. It will be found that not only the clergy but laymen also who are entitled to it sign " Master " before their names in the seventeenth century. Not invariably but usually Robert Bruce's autograph is prefixed by the " Master."[1]

Bruce was about seventeen years of age when he went abroad to France, whence he proceeded to the great Belgian College of Louvain. We have no details of the journey, or of the life abroad, save in a general way. In his Diary of a later date Bruce admits that he was subject to sea-sickness, so that, like James Melville in similar circumstances, he may have suffered from this cause when on his way to France. The passage was indeed a serious undertaking at the period: " The rascality of custom-house officers, the squalor aboard the boat, sea-sickness, and the terror of pirates made the crossing a veritable nightmare."[2] It is probable that Bruce sailed from the Firth of Forth, as he certainly did on a voyage to France in the year 1600. In a letter written years after he tells us that he had suffered bad health when abroad as a student.[3] It is probable that he went reluctant, and only in deference to his parents' desire, following the pursuit of law in the crowded continental universities, while a great portion of his affections was already engaged to the Reformers in Scotland. All the while he studied he was haunted by the dread that he went counter to the will of God.

The schools of France were and had been for fifty years the resort of Scottish students of law. Sir Thomas Craig, after-

---

[1] See Laing's *Works of John Knox*, vol. i., Appendix No. 14, p. 556.
[2] Erasmus, quoted in Hume Brown's *Scotland in the Time of Queen Mary*, p. 70.
[3] Wodrow's *Life of Bruce*, p. 94.

wards a distinguished member of the College of Justice, pursued the study of law at Paris about the year 1555. The power of this great university may be estimated when it is told that thirty thousand students attended it in one year. The education of those Scottish youths who studied the law usually culminated in a tour through the Continent. Thereafter they spent some time in " haunting the forms and courts," that they might acquire a practical acquaintance with the forms of procedure, being in due course admitted advocates.[1]

It may have been to obtain a deeper acquaintance with civil law, which had been prohibited by Papal Bull at the University of Paris, that Bruce turned his face towards the Belgian University of Louvain. It is significant that this last university was a centre and rallying-point of anti-Reformation learning, and Scottish folk cannot forget that a letter was sent from Louvain giving approval of the burning of Patrick Hamilton.[2] Concerning the student life at Louvain, there are minute details bearing upon the year 1476. It is probable that in so conservative a stronghold there would be little change in the succeeding hundred years, so that it may be worth while to supply details of the life at that college a century before Master Robert Bruce entered its class-rooms. There were six thousand students enrolled in this famous centre of learning in a single year. A graduate of one university was " free " of all,[3] so that Bruce's St. Andrews " pass " would stand him in good stead. He would find himself drawn towards the group of Scottish students, and his natural bent to study and serious thought, as well as his social connections, would place him among the best men. Lectures were delivered in Latin, the mediæval usage still obtaining. Bruce was a Latin scholar, owing a deep debt, like Knox, to the great theologian Augustine. We shall find later on that, as with others of the same training, his very dreams took their form in the Latin tongue.[4]

Among the students of Louvain there were, of course, many sorts: careless and licentious men, but also devout, earnest

[1] Tytler's *Life of Sir T. Craig*, pp. 8-22.   [2] Cald., vol. i. p. 80.
[3] C. Innes, *Early Scottish History*, p. 281.   [4] See p. 280.

scholars. It was the duty of their tutors to rouse these young men out of bed at 5 a.m. Under careful supervision they spent their day listening to lecture, revising, committing to memory. Every hour was accounted for, brief intervals being allowed for meals or recreation. In the evening, when work was over, the "honestum jocum" was admitted. Unhappily, even under so strict regulations the wilder spirits found opportunity for excess.

On his return to Scotland Bruce commenced the practice of law in the Court of Session, and he had a prospect through family influence of gaining speedy admission to the College of Justice. This college, instituted by James V. for the purpose of procuring "ane permanent ordour of justice," was composed of fifteen men, seven of whom were chosen from the temporal estate and eight from the spiritual order. These senators were possessed of high privileges.[1] In order to qualify his son for his promotion to this great position, Sir Alexander Bruce put him in possession of the estate of Kinnaird adjoining his own lands. It becomes clear, however, about this point, that the struggle of soul through which for years young Bruce has been passing is about to come to a head. The very process by which, solely through family influence, it was proposed to put the young man upon this bench of senators, may have shocked his sensitive nature and hastened the revolt. It is plain that he shrank from the career which had been marked out for him by his father. On the other hand, Master Robert Bruce had strong leanings towards the profession of the Church. And the moment was come when he must arrive at a decision. There are crises in life wherein every lesser obligation, however sacred, is swallowed up in this one supreme summons of Christ, "Follow Me." This crisis Master Robert recognised that he had to meet. So he took his place among those who have forsaken houses, brethren, sisters, father, mother, wife, children, lands, for the sake of their Lord.

The Narrative of Robert Bruce's great decision upon the night of 31st August 1581 is given with much detail, and the

[1] Tytler's *Life of Craig*, pp. 36-40.

piece ranks with great confessions of the soul, such as those of
Pascal or Bunyan.[1] He informs us frankly that the hands
which held him back from the path to which he felt himself
summoned by God were those of his own mother. The laird,
easy-going as he was, after a little hesitation consented to his
student son joining the Melvilles for the study of theology. But
the Roman Catholic mother withheld her permission until he
should surrender the estate of Kinnaird and his other possessions. "And that I did willingly; cast my clothes from me, my
vain and glorious apparel, sent my horse to the fair, and emp-
tied my hands of all."

There are two outstanding episodes that reveal to us vividly
the ordeal of those days of suspense. One of these is the conversation, during a walk in the fields at St. Andrews, between
Bruce and James Melville, his former fellow-student of undergraduate days. It was in the course of a frank and brotherly
talk with this friend that Bruce confided to him how, rather than
cast himself again into the agony of conscience which he had
endured for resisting the call of God into the Christian ministry,
he would rather go through a fire of brimstone half a mile long.
Bold words these—words which, if he be willing to carry out in
practice, must make of him a force of the first rank in the
Church!

The other incident connects itself with the old Castle of Airth,
and is earlier in time. "When I was a young man," Bruce
told a Christian friend in the time of his old age, "I lived by
faith in the Son of God." In his Narrative Master Robert
writes: "I was first called to my grace, before I obeyed my
calling to the ministry: He made me first a Christian before
He made me a minister. I resisted long my calling to the
ministry: ten years at least I never leaped on horseback nor
alighted, but with a justly accusing conscience." Thereupon in
a passage which reminds one of Bunyan's *Grace Abounding*
for the depths of its colouring, he describes a night ne'er to be
forgotten by him, the 31st August 1581, when he lay in his bed,
side by side with some "brother of the ministry," whose name

[1] Cald., iv. pp. 635-638.

he considerately withholds. They were accustomed three hundred years ago to sleep two and two. Master Robert was unfortunate in his companion, whom he roused, and asked his aid, but despite his calling he had no word in him of help. " I recommended my dolorous estate to his prayers, but I found him a comfortless comforter." So this man of an anxious spirit must fight his way, Luther-like, alone in the night. Is it to be wondered at, if never afterwards he could forget the place, the year, the day?

But he must tell his own story. It is far too precious to be curtailed. " At last it pleased God, in the year 1581, in the month of August, in the last night thereof, being in the Place of Airth, lying in a chamber called the New Loft Chamber, in the very while I lay, to cite me inwardly, judicially in my conscience, and to present all my sins before me in such sort that He omitted not a circumstance, but made my conscience to see time, place, persons as vividly as in the hour I did them. He made the devil to accuse me so audibly that I heard his voice as vividly as ever I heard anything, not being asleep but awake. And so far as he spake true, my conscience bare him record, and testified against me very clearly. But when he came to be a false accuser, and laid things to my charge which I had never done, then my conscience failed him and would not testify with him. And in these things that were true my conscience condemned me, and the accuser himself tormented me, and made me feel the wroth of God pressing me down as it were to the lower hell. Yea, I was so fearfully and extremely tormented that I would have been content to have been cast into a cauldron of hot melted lead, to have had my soul relieved of that insupportable weight. Always, so far as he spoke true, I confessed, restored God to His glory, and craved God's mercy for the merits of Christ: yea, appealed sore to His mercy, purchased to me by the blood, death, and passion of Christ. This court of justice " (mark the legal terminology of the young Scotch jurist!) " holden upon my soul, turned of the bottomless mercy of God into a Court of Mercy to me: for that same night, ere the day dawned or ever the sun rose, He restrained these furies, and these outcries of my justly accusing conscience, and enabled me to rise in the morning."

The particular colour of a Christian teacher's message will always be affected by his experiences in the great process of his observation. Bruce himself points to this " visitation " as the " first motion that chased " him to grace. And we will not be surprised to find that one who passed through a struggle, protracted and painful like that of which this passage given above supplies the crisis, became a great master of the conscience in his ministry. Bruce was much sought after as a leech skilful in the cure of souls, and those sermons of his which remain reveal a man whose message was searching, yet kindly, so as to heal the broken in heart.

CHAPTER III

A Student of Theology at the New College

SOME critics will be ready to pronounce this frank confession of Robert Bruce morbid and unhealthy; the extraordinary disclosure of subjective conditions may not be to their mind. But Bruce's after-life, all of a piece with the conversion of 31st August, is a sufficient answer. The long, consistent career of the minister, Bruce, is as much the outcome of that experience in the chamber of Airth Castle as St. Paul's missionary life was the outcome of his vision on the way to Damascus.

Others there are who will declare that what occurred in Robert Bruce's spirit was due to bodily illness. And undoubtedly, in any disturbance of this kind, a scientific treatment must take into account not only the spiritual but the bodily conditions. There is a pathology of our complex human nature which must be considered by every physician of souls. Bruce himself mentions that he suffered from broken health when abroad, and he traces its origin to spiritual distress.[1] This physical condition is certainly turned in many instances to highest religious purpose by the divine overruling. Ill-health has often been a means of sending the soul back upon itself and upon God. And the sickroom becomes a place of prayer and of real repentance.

Bruce and his friends make quite clear that the suspense endured by the sufferer was seriously undermining a constitution never robust: " I resolved," he writes, " to go to St. Andrews to Master Andrew Melville, and there to lay out my doleance in his bosom, and to communicate all my griefs with him. It was

[1] Wodrow's *Life of Bruce*, p. 94; Cald., iv. p. 18; Melville's *Diary*, p. 147.

27

long before I could get leave to go. My mother made me such an impediment. My father at last consented, but my mother would not, till I had denuded my hands of some lands and casualities I was infeft in." And the testimony of James Melville agrees: "He (Bruce) was fain at last plainly to show his father that there was neither rest nor life for him until he had leave to go to the study of theology, and be in company with Master Andrew Melville in St. Andrews."[1]

Between the year 1581, when Bruce was converted, and the year 1583, when he reappears in St. Andrews University, there occur two years concerning which we have no information. What was Bruce doing in the interval? They may have been years in which, like St. Paul in Arabia,[2] he retired that he might meditate and allow his resolve to mature. We can picture him brooding in some solitude upon the future, forming a policy, studying the problems which beset his country. Certainly, when he embarked upon his more public life he was a man with his mind entirely made up. The melancholy reluctance of those of his own home would naturally make him more deliberate in his advance, so that two more years went by, and Bruce had attained to the ripe age of nine-and-twenty ere he entered upon the study of theology at the College of St. Mary's.

The College of St. Mary's into which with so ill a grace Master Robert Bruce was permitted to enter, was part of the famous University of St. Andrews, the light of which had now burned high for a century and a half upon the east coast of Scotland. The reorganising of St. Andrews University had just taken place. We must know that, as this was the oldest, so it was the most important of the four Scottish universities, both in revenue and in the number of students who frequented it. St. Mary's, commonly known as the New College, in contrast with St. Salvator's or the Auld College, was now converted entirely into a School of Divinity, with five professorships, one of these being for the study of Hebrew. Andrew Melville was called by the voice of all Scotland to be the principal of this new Theological

---

[1] Melville's *Diary*, p. 147.   [2] Galat. i. 17, 18.

College.[1] He had entered St. Mary's as a student at the tender age of fourteen, and now he was called back to preside over it under the new condition. When Melville in 1559 came first to St. Mary's, Greek and Hebrew were unknown there, and the professors were amazed to find that this youthful prodigy could read Aristotle in the Greek text. Andrew Melville had acquired his accomplishment in Montrose, at the hands of a learned Frenchman who was master there. The language in common use was of course Latin. Everyone admitted to the ministry of the Church must know the Latin language, unless he had some distinguishing degree of natural gifts and of piety, when an exception might be made. Scholars of the seventeenth century spoke fluently and thought in Latin. They actually dreamed in the Latin of the monks and of the Vulgate. One Scotsman remained so long in the mediæval atmosphere of foreign universities that on his return home he found that he had forgotten his native language altogether.

James Melville, the Diarist, mentions that on his entering St. Leonard's College in 1571 (1569) he was much chagrined to find himself, on account of defective schooling, quite unable to understand the lectures which were delivered in Latin, and that he burst into tears before the whole class. The same James Melville made, however, such rapid progress that in 1581 he returned to St. Andrews as a teacher, and found himself instructing in the Hebrew tongue men who had been masters and regents when he was a scholar. To his gracious pen we owe a richly coloured picture of the life at the New College under the direction of his distinguished uncle, Andrew Melville. We are admitted to the modest chambers of undergraduates and to the crowded lecture hall; we overhear the quarrels and perceive the jealousies which divide that community; we are permitted to see them that pursue golf or archery, as well as those more serious men who aim at scholarship. A fire that threatens to burn down the college is with difficulty extinguished; a guest on his departure narrowly misses death by drowning; the bishop, lying like a fox in his den, consults witchcraft for his cure. All the

[1] M'Crie's *Melville*, pp. 73-75.

burdens and triumphs of this community of students are depicted for us with a masterly skilfulness of delineation by the
Diarist, James Melville.

Into this distinctly narrow and exclusive community Robert
Bruce entered in the autumn of 1583, when an instantaneous
friendship, such as is commonly cemented between young men
of like tastes and prejudices, was formed between the young
student of theology and James Melville, who must have been
the very youngest of the professors. That winter session in St.
Andrews was a memorable one in many respects. It was the
custom for students of the Theological College to take their turn
in expounding Scripture, both on the week-days and on Sundays, the public being admitted upon the latter occasions.
Bruce, though he must have been in years one of the senior
men, was so bashful and oppressed with shame and blushing
that he could not be induced to take his turn as expounder. He
begged rather to be heard privately in the presence of a few
friends. So, gradually gaining confidence, he made bold to expound the Epistle to the Hebrews at the students' exercise; and
ere long he ventured to preach on Sunday mornings, with the
result that the inhabitants of the city crowded to his service,
deserting King James' archbishop, who held forth in the city
church.[1]

"So it pleased God," James Melville writes piously, "at that
time, to my singular support and encouragement in His service,
to begin to train up and mould that most notable preacher for
the time of restitution of His decayed and captive Jerusalem."

Andrew Melville, if since the death of George Buchanan he
ranked as the most scholarly man in Scotland, was at the same
time an antagonist who allowed himself to use great boldness of
speech. Not his most devoted admirers can call him a courtier;
even before his King he had a Knox-like way of calling a fig a
fig and a spade a spade. Whether in the pulpit or in the palace,
he was ready to speak out his mind without fear. In a sermon
which he preached on the occasion of a fast it was alleged that
he had attacked King James; and in the spring of 1584, before

[1] Melville's *Diary*, pp. 147, 148.

the college session was over, he found himself summoned to appear before the King's Privy Council at Edinburgh, to answer to a charge of treason. But from the first it was clear that the object of King James' advisers in making this charge was to silence Andrew Melville's powerful voice, and if possible to remove from his position in St. Andrews the most formidable opponent of their ecclesiastical policy.

Modern students of this period of Scottish history, even when they may be in full sympathy with the Melville party in their vindication of religious and civil liberty, will feel that the language in which the Reformers addressed the people was unnecessarily provocative. Their daring introduction of politics into the pulpit, their indulgence in personalities, must, we often feel, have injured their own cause, and surely a little more tact and prudence would have been seemly. On the other hand, their own age alone should in fairness be their judge in matters of taste. We are not entitled to subject the people who lived three hundred years ago to the test of our present standards. It was use and wont to bring all matters of immediate public interest to the pulpit. The ministry were guides of public opinion, not only on strictly religious, but on social and even political questions. Excommunication was still a tremendous menace in the social world. The clergy and the Church wielded a power such as is to-day in the hands of the civil magistrate.

Nor must it be forgotten that in those years, wherein the echoes of Knox's voice had scarce yet died away, the people were jealous of their liberty, which had lately been purchased at a great price from the dominion of Rome. Their horror lest that intolerable yoke should be placed again upon their necks begot in them a vigilance and an outspokenness with which everyone who has apprehended the suffering through which the nation passed into her freedom can fully sympathise.

Alongside of Andrew Melville, as he entered Edinburgh to answer for his language, there stood several of his scholars and friends, amongst them Robert Bruce.[1] This was the first baptism of the young St. Andrews student into those trials of which

---

[1] Melville's *Diary*, p. 141.

his after-life was full. The university furnished Melville with a vigorous attestation of his innocence of the charges laid against him. "We, Rector, deans, professors, regents, masters, within the University of St. Andrews, convened together in the fear of God, after calling upon His name, have thought it meet to send forth this our testimony by our commissioners appointed for that effect, Master Robert Bruce, Master Robert Wilkie, . . . to your Majesty and Honourable Counsel, that whatsoever is laid to our brother's charge, so long as he occupied the chair of verity and place in schools within this city, as it is false and feigned in itself, so it is only forged of the devil and his instruments to bring the faithful servants of God into contempt and hatred of their Supreme Magistrate (King James); which God forbid!"[1] The "testimonial," as it is called, of which the above is a pithy portion, bears evidence that it is Bruce's handiwork, and his name stands foremost on the list of those who presented it to the Privy Council. It was his first public act, and in taking this step he committed himself to the party with which his name became afterwards identified. He was present, a quiet specta-tor, during all that brilliant sequel, which every historian describes, when Melville, fearless and gay-hearted like a soldier marching to battle, faced his accusers; and when the great scholar finally took his little Hebrew Bible from his belt and, "clanking it down upon the table before the King," and before the favourite, Captain James Stewart, said, "there is my in-struction and warrant; let me see which of you can judge there-on, or control me therein, that I have exceeded my orders, . . . I stand for the cause of Christ and His Kirk."[2]

Bruce would not fail to take the measure of those proceedings which ensued; the production of one who became Melville's "accuser" (indeed, the ignominious name attached to him for many years thereafter); the introduction of witnesses—Melville's "greatest mislikers"—out of St. Andrews; finally, the unjust sentence, that for his irreverent behaviour in the presence of His Majesty and the Council, Melville should be put in ward in the Castle of Edinburgh during the King's will.

[1] Cald., iv. p. 4.   [2] Melville's *Diary*, p. 142.

This sentence was somehow altered to the more severe one of detention at the Castle of Blackness, "a foul hole keepit by Captain James' men," situated on the shores of West Lothian not far from Linlithgow. This was the dungeon afterwards made notorious by the imprisonment within it of half a dozen of the most steadfast ministers. During the brief interval which lay between the trial and the enforcing of the sentence Melville continued in the city among his friends, but the shadow of the "foul hole" on the coast lay heavy upon their company. There is a description of a dinner-party at Master James Lawson's manse up in the High Street, where Bruce must have been one of the guests, as his comrade James Melville was. It is this last who tells the story. The company were very grave and sad. Lawson, the host, Knox's successor in St. Giles pulpit, is described as a melancholian in constitution, and his temper affected all the rest. They "mixed their tears with their drink," as they brooded over the imminent loss of such a light and leader as Andrew Melville. It is not likely that any of them could foretell that day how upon the death of Lawson (which occurred a few months after, and was hastened through the hardships which he encountered) the quiet student of theology, Robert Bruce, should succeed him in the occupancy of Knox's pulpit. When Melville entered the dining-room, however, there was a change in the demeanour of the guests. He brought with him an infectious gaiety and a light-heartedness which lifted the gloom. As his custom was at meals and in company, he talked of public matters, interspersing the conversation with many a quip and merry tale, so that everyone caught the infection of his humour. A true captain this, as the *Diary* pictures him,[1] of the armies of the Church. Little wonder that he had disciples, and that when he was sent into exile good men and true sprang up to testify in his stead. That same night, accompanied by his brother Roger, he slipped out of the city gate, and within twenty-four hours was safe across the border at Berwick.

At St. Andrews the burden of administration rested, in the

[1] Melville's *Diary*, p. 144.

B

absence of Melville, upon his nephew the Diarist, a man of strong convictions, but of gentler nature than the other. Among his supports at this crisis he mentions, as his special daily friend and companion, Master Robert Bruce. In addition to the class-work, his share of which in the absence of his uncle was greatly increased, he undertook the care of the finances of the college, which were subjected at this time to a severe strain. In the management of these Bruce's business training was found in-valuable, and with much patient care he assisted James Melville in all his transactions.

In the midst of all these academic cares a more public question loomed up large before the Reformers, who were now with-out their leader. A series of measures was enacted by Parlia-ment, known to the Reformation party as the Black Acts, by which all that Melville and his friends had been patiently build-ing up with a view to the Church's liberty was by a stroke over-thrown. These Acts denied to the Church any right of assem-bly, save by royal permission; the order of bishops was restored in every part of the kingdom; to decline the judgment of his Majesty or of the Privy Council in any matter was declared to be treason; to pass any contemptuous criticism upon the King was an offence to be punished with great severity. Against those Acts of Parliament the sturdy ministers of St. Giles—Bal-canquhal, Lawson, and Pont—publicly protested at the Mercat Cross of Edinburgh. This bold action resulted in the instant issue of orders for their arrest. Lawson distinguished himself by bold public remonstrances on account of the treatment to which Melville had been subjected by the Privy Council, and in consequence he was the object of Captain James Stewart's peculiar aversion. The chancellor was heard to declare, "that if Master James Lawson's head were as great as a haystack he would cause it to leap from his shoulders." Upon this Lawson and his brethren discreetly made their way across the border to Berwick.

James Melville, at his post of duty in St. Andrews, was very unwilling to flee. However, an uncle of his, who was also an inti-mate friend of Bruce, the same Roger Melville who had escorted

Master Andrew through the city port, came over hastily on the Sabbath from Dundee with serious news. There was a writ issued to search Master James Melville's house and to seize his person.

James Melville was a man who, for all his mild manners, had a will of his own, and his worthy Dundee kinsman found "it difficult to persuade him to desert his post." But Roger was a man of resources. He is the man of whom Robert Bruce was wont to say that if he had enjoyed the education of Andrew Melville, his brother, he would have been the most *singular* man in Europe. He was a person of marked piety, and a citizen of large influence in his own town. His position would give him early access to information, and in great alarm he hastened to warn his nephew, bringing to bear on him not only his own influence but that of Bruce, who joined his entreaties to those of the other, that James Melville should take to flight. At length he yielded to their united supplication, and by a hasty withdrawal that same Sabbath evening to Dundee he was able to avoid arrest and imprisonment. The story of his escape in an open boat from the port of Dundee to Berwick; of his pulling personally at an oar "till the hide came off his fingers"; of his conducting devotions on board, in which one sailor who was evil-affected refused to join; of the chattering of sea-birds on the crag of St. Abbs, angry because their young were disturbed by the passing boat; of the mist that came down, and protected God's servant; of his final arrival out of many perils of waters in the haven of Berwick—all this and more may be read in the graphic pages of James Melville.[1]

[1] *Diary*, pp. 168-170.

CHAPTER IV

Bruce's Response to a Call from Edinburgh

NOTHING has been discovered as to the occupations of Master Robert Bruce during the two years which followed, 1584-1586. The descent of a scourge of plague upon Scotland flung the whole country into confusion, affecting the University of St. Andrews, scattering the students, disorganising the colleges. Adamson, that feeble sycophant on whom King James had bestowed the title Archbishop of St. Andrews, made an attempt to guide the university in the absence of Andrew Melville. The students, however, being naturally on the side of their banished principal, resented his interference, and met his advances with petty acts of annoyance—such horseplay as students to this very day know how to indulge in. The result was that the insulted archbishop left St. Andrews in high dudgeon. It is probable also that Bruce about this time retired from the desolate College of St. Mary's to his beautiful family home of Airth. There, hard by the banks of Forth, one pictures him moving amongst his kinsfolk, studying his favourite books, finding leisure time to mature his reflections upon both theology and life. The teaching which he had imbibed at St. Andrews would during this placid interval have opportunity to mature.

We cannot enlarge in these pages upon such questions as belong to history in the larger sense of the word. Suffice it to say, that the young King was under the dominion of a favourite, James Stewart, who led him upon a wild and vicious course, till at length a reaction set in, and those noblemen whom the policy of King James had estranged were restored to the direction of affairs. In their train the Melville party were summoned back to their posts, and by the year 1586 the University

of St. Andrews was on the way to recover itself. The plague
was by this time spent, but in the *Diary* of James Melville we
have a graphic picture of the desolation which was spread over
the land as a consequence of its ravages. " I miskenned Edinburgh, and almost forgot that ever I had seen sic a town."[1] It
was considered by the people that the hand of God was in all
this, and that " the pest would not abate till the ministers of
God and noblemen were brought home again." That sombre
view of the origin of the pestilence coloured the entire thinking
of the time. The message of every earnest preacher was affected
by the memory of this dread divine scourge. And it was remarked by keen observers that, on the replacing in their posts
of those good men who had been expatriated, the pest forthwith
abated and began to be withdrawn by the merciful hand of God,
so that Edinburgh was frequented again that winter. " On the
return of spring all the towns, almost desolate before, were re-
peopled, St. Andrews among the rest: to the which Master
Andrew Melville and I returned and entered into the college
about the middle of the month of March."[2]

It may be worth while to describe a sermon preached by
James Melville at the opening of the Fife Synod in April 1586.
No one has ever accused the younger Melville of lack of courtesy
or of rudeness of speech. He was, as the *Diary* on every page
of it unconsciously reveals, a chivalrous gentleman as well as a
Christian of real charm of character. It was this man who,
acting on behalf of the greatest Provincial Synod of the Church,
as spokesman of her policy, turned in the course of his sermon
to Archbishop Adamson, who had taken his seat with great
pomp by the preacher's side, and in stinging words drew attention to his tortuous public career. " I take the Synod to witness," said he, "and your own conscience before God, that
being a minister of the Kirk you have become poisoned with
avarice and ambition and will ruin the whole Body, in case you
are not timeously and with courage cut off." Thereupon the
Synod was exhorted to play the surgeon's part for preserving
of the Body, seeing that " all means of amendment had been

[1] Melville's *Diary*, p. 228.   [2] *Ibid.*, p. 245.

tried in vain upon that most corrupt and monstrous member."[1]

While it should be added that the more outspoken uncle, Andrew Melville, had chosen the text that day, and may have inspired the argument, it is a fact that all the brethren approved, and proceeded to excommunicate Adamson. Other days, other manners. And it would be impertinent, as it would be unhistorical on our part, to censure the Moderator's language or his discourse. When, later on, we shall hear Master Robert Bruce, in the pulpit of St. Giles, speaking out with the same breadth of language, we must remember that in this respect he was a child of his own age. Readers of Bruce's sermons will find that when the King was in the royal pew the preacher was wont to pay his Majesty the compliment of singling him out for a direct exhortation. During the preaching of the first sermon upon Isaiah xxxviii, the King, as we are told in the title of it, was present. Towards the end Bruce proceeds: " But specially the Lord make you, Sir, so to walk in your life that you may have a joyful testimony of your conscience in your death."[2] The following curious incident is far too well authenticated to be dismissed. One day the King was seated in his gallery, surrounded by several courtiers, while Bruce preached. James was notoriously rude during divine service, and on this occasion he began, as frequently happened, to talk to those about him while the sermon proceeded. Bruce paused, and the King fell silent, but upon the minister resuming he was guilty of a second interruption, which was checked in the same way. A third time the King offended; whereupon Bruce turned to him and spoke: " It is said to have been an expression of the wisest of kings, 'When the lion roars, all the beasts of the field are quiet': the Lion of the Tribe of Judah is now roaring in the voice of His Gospel, and it becomes all the petty kings of the earth to be silent."[3]

From this it is evident that Bruce was no court preacher. But let not the modern reader take offence with his style. Those were times of strong measures and strong men. Perhaps a

---

[1] Melville's *Diary*, p. 246.   [2] Wodrow's *Bruce*, p. 176.
[3] Livingstone. See Wodrow's *Bruce*, p. 154.

future generation, more robust than ours, may call the men of to-day dilettante and effeminate.

The session of 1586-87 was a memorable one at St. Andrews. The two Melvilles were at their desks; the class-rooms were again thronged with students; not only was the study of theology resumed, but those religious services were revived which had become a leading feature of the university under the principalship of Andrew Melville. There was a curious contest for possession of the ear of the city between Bruce and Melville on the one side, and Archbishop Adamson on the other.

As for the latter, his ministrations had a certain piquancy among the people, partly through his being excommunicate, partly that he was known to have the covert support of King James. Add to this the attraction of Adamson's "pleasant utterance," and it will be understood how many people found their way to the parish church when he conducted service. The best people, however, both of town and university, had scruples about worshipping under him, and resorted in large numbers to the chapel of the New College, where Robert Bruce and Andrew Melville preached every Sabbath to their great edification.[1] For the former of these men this year 1586 may be counted the beginning of his public ministry. By this time he had evidently overcome that "bashfulness and blushing" of which he speaks in the narrative composed in his old age. "God opened his mouth at that time," as the pious Church historian remarks,[2] and soon it was evident that a force of the first rank was at the disposal of the Church in the person of Bruce.

At this point we can again take up our tale in the pages of that too brief narrative, Bruce's own notes of his life, which he composed when he was old. It was Andrew Melville who designated Bruce for the succession in Knox's church of St. Giles, Edinburgh. "Master Andrew took me over with him" to the Assembly held in Edinburgh, June 1587. "Edinburgh lacked pastors, and they made a leet of some, . . . putting in my name among the rest. They would have me teach among the rest, and after long entreaty I consented, and taught upon the

[1] Melville's *Diary*, p. 254.   [2] Cald., iv. p. 586.

spiritual armour, Eph. vi. In a crowded Assembly the leets
came up for decision, who should be chosen. I remember Mr.
Udall, the Englishman "[1] (a well-known Puritan who had
suffered much for his convictions), " was there, and sundry
other strangers. Surely, with universal consent, very few excepted, I am chosen and appointed."

Master Robert, in the narrative of his old age, was entitled to
indulge in those pleasing reminiscences. For it was a splendid
situation in which the high confidence of his masters as well
as his own preaching gift placed him while he was still a probationer. It is to be kept in mind, however, that Bruce was
mature and experienced far beyond his thirty years. He was
more: he was not to be readily swayed by the judgment of other
men; and his " native obstinacy," to borrow a phrase of Calderwood, as it was to baffle his foes in after years, perplexed his
most intimate friends in the matter of the call to be minister of
St. Giles. Not even the united entreaty of the two Melvilles
could shake him in his purpose of refusal. He is very com-
municative about the matter. He has another " call " in his
hands, very hearty, supported by both kirk and college, to be
minister of St. Andrews. " And surely I liked better to go to
St. Andrews, for I had no taste for preaching before the Court,"
as would be necessary in St. Giles. " For well I knew that the
Court and we could never agree."[2] Master Robert knew by this
time that he had a tongue which could not flatter, and that he
dared not withhold the truth even in the presence of kings. In
the end he had his way, and went back across the Firth of Forth
to his former post. However, it was not easy to be quit of the
claims of the capital. A formidable deputation crossed over
the ferry in pursuit of the man upon whom Edinburgh had set
its heart. " Loath was I to go: they threatened me with
authority. So I advised with my God, and thought it meet
to obey."

At this point another aspect of Master Robert's character is
disclosed, and one which marks him out as exceptional among

[1] John Udall, see p. 42.
[2] Bruce's Narrative, quoted, Cald., iv. p. 637.

the men of his time. Not only was he reluctant, with the noble reluctance of an Old Testament prophet, to undertake the heavy charge of souls in Edinburgh, but he tells us that he was assailed with doubts of an intellectual sort, such as must have been unusual in his century. A credible witness makes this statement, mentioning that Bruce had sore scruples of the mind, being assaulted especially with doubts upon the foundation truth whether there is a God over all; doubts which cost him days and nights of agony. On entering the pulpit, after engaging a while in silent prayer, he would lift up his head and say sometimes, " I think it a great matter to believe that there is a God," adding that it was quite another matter to believe than people thought.[1]

Those were some of the grounds upon which Master Robert, while unwillingly consenting to teach in the church of St. Giles, and assay how the Lord would bless his labours, firmly refused to submit to the ordeal of ordination. His hesitation was by no means due to some whim. Years afterwards when confined by the cruel orders of his King to Inverness, he imparted deliberately to a visitor from a large book which he had composed the tale of those hard and sore exercises which his soul had met with both before his entry to the ministry at Edinburgh and after; as also the strong consolations whereby the Lord had comforted him.[2] That " large book," which if it were forthcoming would be worthy of a niche in our collections of great literature beside Bunyan's *Grace Abounding* and Augustine's *Confessions*, is lost, but the visitor (who was a student of theology) wrote down what had been quoted. " I found within me," says the narrative already referred to, " such a mountain of iniquity, dividing between His Majesty's comfortable presence and me, that I thought it was not His Majesty's pleasure that I should take the full burden on me till the impediment were removed."[3]

Two years later the congregation of St. Andrews made

[1] Fleming, *Fulfilling of Scripture*, vol. i. p. 366.
[2] Blair's *Autobiography*, Wodrow, p. 39.
[3] Bruce's Narrative, quoted, Cald., iv. p. 638. " His Majesty " here, as often in Bruce's sermons, refers to God. The King is usually " his Highness," or " his Majesty."

another effort to secure Master Robert, to which action they were no doubt encouraged by the minister's refusal to be tied to the Edinburgh charge by the bond of ordination. The curious student may still read upon the register of St. Andrews Kirk-Session, 7th May 1589, how the members of that charge with one voice, after earnest calling on the holy name of God, elected and chose Master Robert Bruce, as a man most meet, able, and qualified to be minister and fellow-labourer with Master Robert Wilkie. " And commissioners from town, university, and parish have agreed with all diligence, in the most fervent manner, to invite the said Master Robert Bruce to come and occupy the office conform to free election."[1] But it was all in vain. For well-nigh twelve years Bruce maintained his testimony without interruption in Edinburgh, and Melville's confidence in his favourite student was amply justified. Reluctant as he was to take up the burden, Bruce was, if possible, even more reluctant to lay it down.

NOTE TO CHAPTER IV

John Udall, mentioned on page 40, was an English Puritan. He preached before the King and the General Assembly, 1589 (Cald., v. p. 58). Later, he suffered for his hostility to Episcopacy, and a letter may be read (Cald., v. p. 132) which is from Bruce's pen (Quick in the *Icones* ascribes the letter to Bruce) remonstrating with Queen Elizabeth for her treatment of the Puritan minister. This letter was sent by a Mr. Johnson, a Scottish merchant, to London, and by him presented to the Queen, perused by her Majesty, and remitted to the Privy Council (Fuller, *Hist.*, iii. p. 113). In Fuller's references the persecution of Cartwright and certain other ministers is also referred to. Cartwright is the same who refused the divinity chair at St. Andrews, 1584. On the whole, we can trace here an instance of Bruce's deep sympathy with the English Puritans, a sympathy which the case of Mrs. Drake (p. 174) further illustrates. Bruce was evidently well known to the English

[1] Hay Fleming's *Published Register of St. Andrews Kirk Session*, part ii. p. 640.

Puritans; his sermons were popular among them (p. 78), and he is chosen (with John Welsh) as one of two Scottish confessors who find a place among the Worthies in Quick's *Icones*.[1] His interposition on behalf of John Udall was to no purpose; condemned to be executed, the faithful man died in prison ere the sentence of death could be carried out.

[1] Quick's *Icones Sacræ Anglicanæ:* an unpublished MS. volume; Biographies of Leading Nonconformists. Dr. Williams' Library, London.

CHAPTER V

A Great Ministry in the Kirk of St. Giles

THE public life of Master Robert Bruce in the city of Edinburgh was cast in troublous times. His ministry in the Church of St. Giles had an influence which was quite unique, and the voice which found utterance in the capital had its echo throughout the whole Church. There were circumstances in Bruce's previous career which prepared him for the great position in which he found himself. His great social position was in his favour; the breadth and variety of his training gave him exceptional advantage; above all things, he had his mind made up with reference to critical public questions, and there was on him the stamp of a true messenger of Jesus Christ. " The godly for his puissant and most moving doctrine loved him; the worldly for his parentage and place reverenced him, and the enemies for both stood in awe of him."[1] It was felt that a successor to Knox had been raised up in Providence.

In the very first twelvemonth of his pastorate, February 1588, Bruce found himself thrust into the chair of Moderator of the General Assembly. The High Court of the Church had been specially summoned, owing to a threatened invasion of the island by Spain. That Bruce was called to preside over its deliberations is a proof that he occupied already a high place in the counsels of the Church.

Let us attempt to bring up to our minds a representation of the preacher and the service in St. Giles Church about the year 1589. As to the aspect of Bruce, it must have been commanding, for in an age which was much less curious about such externals as personal appearance than our own, men spoke of Bruce's countenance and of his calm self-possession when con-

[1] Melville, *Diary*, p. 271.

44

ducting divine service. One close observer, who was resident in Edinburgh, writes: "This day Bruce preached, as he ever doth, very calmly."[1] Men remarked upon his manner in prayer also. He was very brief in prayer when others were present, but every sentence was like a strong bolt shot up to heaven.[2] When deeply exercised in his intercessions he was moved to tears.[3] He had a habit of knocking upon the table with his fingers as he grew importunate in his prayers.[4] To all this should be added the testimony of Kirkton concerning Bruce: "He made always an earthquake upon his hearers, and rarely preached but to a weeping auditory."[5] As in his conduct of the devotions, so in his preaching he tended to brevity. It is a mistake to suppose that our Scottish Reformers were unusually lengthy in their public services. James Melville informs us in the *Diary* that one and a half hours was set as the limit on Sundays, one hour on week-days. In his St. Giles service, at the entry of Queen Anne of Denmark into the capital, Master Robert restricted himself to half an hour. "I shall be short, by God's grace," was a common phrase of this preacher, and another equally pertinent expression was, "By God's grace, I shall make it clear." His anxiety was to be understood: "Ye tak' me up wrong," he interjected in his discourse. Point and lucidity were chief qualities of the great St. Giles minister, Robert Bruce.

On entering the pulpit, it was a habit of Bruce to remain silent a while in secret prayer. "He was no Boanerges as to his voice," remarks a sympathetic worshipper; and, on the contrary, another contemporary speaks of "that trumpet-sound by which the walls of Jericho were overthrown."[6] It is certain that in the Great Church of St. Giles, which even the voice of Knox could but imperfectly fill, Bruce would have had difficulty in

---

[1] *State Papers in the State Paper Office, Scotland,* vol. lxiv. No. 3.
[2] J. Livingstone, "Memorable Characteristics," *Select Biographies,* vol. i. p. 307.
[3] Cald., vi. p. 146.
[4] Fleming, *Fulfilling of Scripture,* i. pp. 366, 367.
[5] Kirkton, *History of the Church,* p. 26.
[6] Scot's *Apol. Narration,* p. 142.

making himself heard. In the last quarter, however, of the six-teenth century that pile of buildings known as St. Giles Church was subdivided into no fewer than four places of worship, in order to accommodate four congregations. These were called the College Kirk, the Great Kirk, the Upper Tolbooth, and the East or Little Kirk. During the years of his Edinburgh minis-try Bruce preached at first in the Great Kirk, ranking as chief minister of Edinburgh. In the later years a series of unhappy events of which he was the victim led to his labours being re-stricted to a smaller congregation, that of North-West Edin-burgh, which met in the Little Kirk. This portion is tradition-ally known as " Master Robert Bruce's Kirk."

At the period of Bruce's entrance on his ministry the lessons for the day would be taken by a reader. Bruce himself gave out the text, and he read it with much solemnity. His very tone and accent quickened his hearers, and there is at least one occasion when his deliberate, solemn repetition of a text from which he was about to preach led to the conversion of one who was present. Bruce would read, not from the Authorised Version (it was not to be published yet for twenty-three years), but from the Geneva Version, which for about eighty years was used in Scotland, before the adoption of the Authorised of 1611. Con-sequently the archaic form of many a quotation from Scripture will strike one; for instance, in the text of the thanksgiving ser-mon for deliverance from the Armada, " Thou art more bright and puissant than the mountains of prey " (Ps. lxxvi. 4). Such unfamiliar words as " daunton," " kythe " or " horologe " (for Isaiah's *sundial*) appear in the sermons. But to our ears the strangest thing of all in the preaching of Master Robert would be his use of the old Scots tongue. The dialect is so hard to be understood to-day that the sermons have been rendered into English for the benefit of modern readers. But this very man-ner of speech was what gave them their power when first they were uttered. Knox was the pioneer of those who cast aside the pedantry of scholastic Latin, and spoke to the people in their homely vernacular. The Scots tongue was spoken by all the nation from King James downwards. And one of the chief

masters of that familiar " vulgar tongue " was Bruce, who deliberately preferred it as a medium. His sermons are without
any of those ornaments of quotation in which his generation
loved to indulge. He preferred great plainness of speech, and
in a preface to the published sermons he apologises for the un-
pretentious language which he uses. " I am somewhat hamely
with you," he remarks in a sermon, in the course of his argument. To-day we can hardly interpret, without a glossary,
words like " throombes " or " leisum " or " bachill," and we are
startled by the recurrence of expressions like " tak tent " or
" spunks of joy," no less than of words like " fash " and
" speir." We may well believe that these sermons are to this
day full of life. They abound in illustrations drawn from political or social incidents of the moment. Figures of speech are
numerous, and they are bold. The preacher can speak of " the
teeth of the soul," meaning that faith which takes hold of
Christ. He proposes to " open his pack and sell some wares,"
or again he seeks to " stanch the bleeding of the cause." He
bids his hearers try themselves by the *square* of God's law, and
he describes Jesus Christ as the *sconce* to which men must flee
for safety. He is as fond of a pithy proverb as Mr. Spurgeon
himself; such as " Ower great wealth gars wit waver," or " They
haud aye still on ae tune." " Is it possible," asks he, " that my
drouth can be slokened with that drink that passed never over
my halse?" In the sermons, along with much simplicity and
point, there is language of great elevation. One meets splendid expressions like this, " A wonderful and miserable madness
that is in the soul of man," or this, " Terrible it is to see the
countenance of God in His justice."[1] Sometimes his thoughts
in the pulpit so move him that he breaks off his argument, and
falls to prayer in the middle of the sermon. In fine, these sermons of Bruce reveal a spirit of the loftiest sort, earnest and
strong; they have that indefinable note of distinction which indicates a master-mind. Soon we are aware, as we read, that
this is a great theologian, whose intellect as well as his heart is
engaged in his work. There is discernible throughout his

[1] Wodrow's *Bruce's Sermons*, p. 207.

preaching a weird note of prognostication, and a cry of coming judgment, all the more surprising when we remember that the preacher is but a youth. The fact is, that these are due to the special time of Bruce's entering upon his ministry in Scotland. All around him he finds laxity, treachery, superstition. " God," cries he, " is not like our countrymen, for they, where they are best known are worst loved; but God, on the contrary, where He is best known He is best loved."

The following extracts may serve to illustrate the lofty and searching thought of Bruce's pulpit discourse:

" It hath been the custom of God from time to time to bring His Church into wonderful extremities, that in the judgment of man there appeareth no hope of safety in them: yea, in our own judgment ofttimes there appeareth no escape. I say it is His custom to bring His Church into these extremities that His glory may appear so much the more in her extraordinary deliverances."

" It is a matter of great consequence to subdue and tame the great idol of evil will. We may speak of it as we please, and say that we are able to do it. But of all the works of the earth it is the greatest. For such is the stubbornness of our will, that it will do nothing but what it liketh itself. The perfection of a Christian standeth in striving; we must either strive, or we shall not be crowned." "That same fury and rage whereby men think to dishonour God and overwhelm His Church, He turneth to the contrary, and maketh out of that same fury His own glory and the deliverance of His Church to shine. The Lord is a wonderful workman. He bringeth about His purpose in such sort that He can draw light out of darkness, and bring forth His own praise out of their greatest rage."

" There are two ways set down in Scripture,—there is a broad and an open way, wherein the proud and vain men of the earth walk; there is a narrow and a strait way wherein the simple, and they that depend on God, walk. The broad way is easy and pleasant in the entry, but the end is everlasting and terrible straitness; the other way is strait in the entry, yet the end is large and pleasant, and bringeth a joyful eternity."

" There remains now, of all these great things, and of all this doctrine which has been taught, but this one lesson. Learn to apply Christ rightly to thy soul, and thou hast won all; thou art a great theologian if thou hast learned this well: for in the right application of Christ to the sick soul, to the wounded conscience, and diseased heart, here begins the fountain of all our felicity and the well-spring of all our joy."[1]

It may help us to enter into the soul of that splendid ministry of the Kirk of St. Giles three hundred years ago if we try to bring before us a special service conducted by Bruce. In the month of October 1588 he conducted a thanksgiving upon two successive Sundays, after the defeat of the Spanish Armada. The proclamation enacted that the service should be followed by holy communion, and accordingly Bruce concludes his discourse with an invitation to " dress for yon table." Those two sermons, preached from Psalm lxxvi., have a special interest as the earliest public utterance of Bruce which has been preserved, and a paragraph or two upon their occasion will be useful.

The Spanish Armada had hung for three years as a menace over Scotland and England. The suspense was tremendous and long drawn out. Rumour had it once and again that the foe was already landed at Dunbar or St. Andrews, "and in very deed," says James Melville, " the Lord of Armies who rides upon the wings of the wind, the keeper of His own Israel, was conveying that monstrous navy about our coasts, and directing their hulks and galleys to the lands, rocks, and sands whereupon He had destined their destruction."[2] Calderwood describes how the invaders were cast upon the Scottish coast, and wandered through the country begging, and found greater clemency and charity than they deserved or expected."[3] Bruce, for his part, had no doubt as to the hand to which the deliverance was due. " As truly," said he, in his emphatic way,—" as truly as the overthrow of Sennacherib, this destruction of the Spaniard was divinely wrought. He thought no

---

[1] *Robert Bruce's Sermons*, by Rev. John Laidlaw, D.D., p. 71, etc.
[2] *Diary*, p. 261.   [3] Cald., *Hist.*, iv. 695.

doubt to have rooted out the Kirk. Yet what cometh to pass,
I pray you? When as he was of mind to combat with the Kirk,
he meeteth with the wind, and he findeth the wind more than
his match, as the carcases of men and of ships in all coasts do
testify." "It is commonly asked, and will be asked to the end
of the world, When was yon great defeat done, and in what
place was yon fleet destroyed? It will be answered again, and
I am assured it is answered already, Yon fleet was destroyed
about the coasts of the Lord's own dwelling-place, where He
made His residence."[1] One must feel thankful that in her hour
of delirious joy over the discomfiture of the Catholic invaders
Scotland had so sure and so clear a guide in St. Giles pulpit.
The mob of High Street and the Canongate were easily ex-
cited in those great old times, and very readily they slipped out
of control. Not on every occasion when they rose was even
Master Robert himself able to keep them in check. But upon
this historic date he was their master. From the window of his
manse he could see that roaring multitude at the cross, who
celebrated the victory in their own fashion. Every mixed
motive his shrewd gaze could take in, as well as all those inferior
passions which were let free. In his sermon at the church no
class of men escaped his scrutiny, from the King himself to the
simplest folk; the timid clergy, the canny merchants of the
Luckenbooths, the law-breakers, all came under the sweep of
his discourse.

If the language was somewhat archaic, what must be said
of certain of the customs which prevailed in the church worship of that elder time? King James had his royal pew in St.
Giles, and he took leave occasionally to interrupt the preacher,
calling his doctrine in question or giving his approbation.
Haughty courtiers might stroll into church noisily, to hear what
was said. Men sat in their pews with their hats on. On one
occasion the following strange episode occurred when Bruce
conducted the service. The lawless, defiant Earl of Bothwell
stepped into church and, kneeling as a penitent, made confes-

sion before all the assembled people of his wicked life, and vowed with tears that he would prove in the future another man. Bruce's exhortation, pointed, searching, dignified, is from the text, " Flee also from the lusts of youth." At the close the miserable nobleman asked the prayers of the assembled congregation; " but soon after he brake out into gross enormities."[1]

Bruce was above all things a preacher to the conscience. He brought his own conscience to bear on all his work. While he took much pains in searching the Scripture, and in preparing his sermons, which indeed bear marks of wide reading among the Fathers, yet the main part of his business lay in " having his soul wrought up to some suitableness of frame."[2] " Of all the diseases that can come on any person," he says in one of the course of sermons on Isaiah, " no question the disease of the soul and conscience is greatest; and of all the diseases and troubles that overtake the conscience, no question this is the greatest, when with the sight of sin, which is enough, and more than enough to any to sustain, when with this sight there is a feeling of God's wrath joined. O then, this sickness is unsupportable, when with the sight of sin is joined a touch and feeling of the wrath of God. Merciful God! if the horror be not exceeding great and terrible, so that it is a wonder if the soul can stand, and is not driven to desperation."

" Is it possible," he asks, out of a deep experience, " that faith and doubting can have place in our soul?" And he defines doubt in memorable terms: " It comprehendeth all the errors, fasheries, stammerings, and wrestlings wherewith our faith is assaulted full oft, which makes us sometimes to despair, sometimes to hope; while we look to ourselves to despair, and while we look on the mercy of God in Christ Jesus, to hope."[3] " The soul must utter such stuff as it hath, to wit, doubting and stammering." But this preacher, out of the depths of his own memorable experience, is assured that doubt is the shadow cast by faith,

[1] Cald., v. p. 68.　　[2] Fleming, *Fulfilling of Scripture*, i. p. 377.
[3] Wodrow's *Bruce's Sermons*, pp. 226, 231, 232.

" Which like a shadow proves the substance true."

" If thy conscience is wounded, assuredly thou shalt doubt. Entertain peace in thy conscience and thou shalt keep faith." Only by strict obedience to the voice of this inward companion can one find relief. " There is not another lesson in Christianity than this : this is the first and the last lesson, to shake off your lusts and affections piece by piece, and so piece by piece renounce thyself that thou mayest embrace Christ."[1] " Renounce myself " is his message. " Looking to the greatness of our misery, and to the greatness of the price whereby He hath redeemed us, what heart is there but would willingly renounce itself to get a part in that redemption?" The tense feeling of his mind in this matter of self-immolation for the sake of his Lord comes out in a story recorded by John Livingstone, who tells us that one day he arrived at Bruce's house to see him, but that it was long ere the other came out of his study. When he came forth all his face was suffused with tears. He said that he had just learnt of the keen suffering of a faithful minister in London for his Lord. " My sorrow is not for him, but for myself," said Bruce; " for had I been faithful like him, I might have got the pillory, and have shed some of my blood for Christ as well as he! but he hath got the crown from us all."[2]

In one of the earliest of those St. Giles sermons the preacher closes with a reference to Romans viii., which sounds the very keynote of his teaching. When Master Robert quotes the splendid " Quis Separabit," he cannot articulate the text of St. Paul as a common preacher might. " We claim Christ as belonging to us, as if no man had a title to Him but we. Our persuasion becomes so strong that we dare at the last to say with the Apostle, What shall separate us from the love of Christ?" And as Bruce, in face of the allurements of those who loved him, or of the menace of those who hated him, stood firm as a tower; so also stood his Master steadfast to him up

---

[1] Wodrow's *Bruce's Sermons*, p. 22
[2] John Livingstone, " Memorable Characteristics," in *Select Biographies*, i. p. 306.

to that supreme hour when, placing his right hand upon the passage from Romans viii., which was his peculiar text and trust, he passed, declaring his faith in the word, "For I am persuaded that neither life nor death shall be able to separate me from the love of God, which is in Christ Jesus our Lord."[1]

Meantime, that right hand is uplifted in St. Giles Church, as the minister pronounces the Doxology with which he was accustomed to end his discourse: "In the righteous merits of Jesus Christ, to whom with the Father and the Holy Ghost be all honour, praise, and glory, for now and ever.—AMEN."

[1] John Livingstone, "Memorable Characteristics," in *Select Biographies*, i. p. 308.

CHAPTER VI

Worthy of a Quarter of the Kingdom

IT must have been about this time that King James VI. first
met his distinguished subject, the minister of St. Giles. The
King worshipped in this church, a certain "loft" or gallery
being assigned for the royal use. In the list of accounts preserved among the archives of St. Giles may be read to this day
the entries of charges made for improving the dingy old interior,
with a view to the better accommodation of King James. These
entries are specially significant about the month of May 1590,
when eager preparations were being made for the home-coming
and the " kirking " of James' youthful bride, Anne of Denmark. The walls were washed and painted, flowers were strewn
upon floor, stalls, and galleries, tapestry was hung in the
aisles. But that romance of the wedding must be narrated
from the beginning.

James the Sixth was at this date twenty-three years of age,
being eight years younger than the minister with whom during
the next decade his career was to be so intimately joined. If
we would estimate fairly the character of James we must take
into account first the great disadvantages of his youth, deprived
as he had been of the influence of both a mother and a father
from his very birth. His guardians provided as they could for
his training, and very high expectations indeed were centred
in him. In the *Diary*, James Melville describes what he calls
the "sweetest sight in Europe," namely, the spectacle of this
boy-king at Stirling, "walking up and down in Auld Lady
Mar's hand, discoursing to my great marvel and astonishment."
The "Auld Lady Mar" and the old George Buchanan, his
tutor, fulfilled their trust to the best of their ability, no doubt,
but it cannot be said that their ward became a credit to them.

Scarcely any figure in all history is more distinctly portrayed than that of the Sixth James; and there is no mistaking his character. Surely it was often with a sense of shame that his fellow-countrymen marked his career—selfish, tortuous, wholly lacking in the more stately attributes of kings. Instead of culture, he had pedantry; when he would be frank, he only succeeded in being coarse; as a substitute for courage, he had recourse to a feline craftiness; he possessed a smattering of scholastic theology, in lieu of a personal faith. In the time of King James the problems that agitated the kingdom were new; the nation had discovered itself, and was far too much united and too self-conscious to submit to what James called his kingcraft. From Tweed to Spey the land was already free, and was exultant in its freedom. The retrograde policy of James, whether in Church or in State, inevitably issued in the ruin of his house, having its culmination upon the scaffold of Whitehall.

It must always be understood that the representatives of the Church in King James' reign were otherwise situated in relation to either King or Parliament, than a Scottish clergyman of the present day. The Church was one of the great estates of Government, more powerful than any " lords spiritual "; whereas the House of Parliament had not yet vindicated for itself the authority which has in later times been associated with that august assemblage. It may be held that the ideals of the Scottish Church were Utopian, and that their claim was preposterous. They certainly were representatives of the needs of their country, and their policy was much more practical than that of their stubborn ruler. The standard which they kept in view was that of the Old Testament. Scotland should be an holy nation, Edinburgh the city of God; politics should be sanctified, and the King, by the grace of God, should become a nursing-father to the Church. No student of these good ministers' actions can doubt their fidelity, and their love for their young sovereign. No subjects ever prayed and hoped more for their King. It may appear intolerable that they should have sent a deputation to the palace enjoining the King to observe family prayers, and to have the Scriptures read at meals. They had great expectations of the young man, expecting that he should be moulded to their ideal. How deep, then, was their chagrin when it became gradually clear to them that James was incorrigible. Such an incident as the following casts a light upon the ministers' attitude to their King far better than many words. John Livingstone heard Master Robert Bruce say, when it was told him that the King lay dying: " I would desire no more for a request than one hour's conference with King James. I know he has a conscience. I made him once weep bitterly in his own house at Holyrood."[1] Fain would the aged servant of God have leapt upon his horse, as he had done once to reach in time the deathbed of Thirlstane, the Chancellor, and have hastened southwards to minister Christian consolations to his dying sovereign. Boyd of Trochrig, another of the Church leaders, said of the King when he heard of his death: " I only wish and hope that the Lord has graciously pardoned his sins and faults, and received him into His heavenly kingdom."[2]

It was meet that King James VI., at the age of three-and-twenty, should bring home to Scotland a consort to share his throne. We read with some surprise his own assurance that he sought guidance in the matter from God, and that after much prayer he was resolved to turn to Denmark for a match.[3] Yet why should not the King seek counsel of God in a matter which would affect greatly both his own life and the happiness of his people? He became for a while romantically in earnest about his marriage, and when the storms, that are no respecters of persons, overtook the fleet which bore his bride to his arms, flinging her back upon her own coasts, the royal wooer took a prompt resolve to set sail for Denmark, and to marry her from her own home. In October 1589 he put out with a goodly retinue, and was absent for six months, during which time he kept up close communications with his capital, having for a correspondent, amongst others, Master Robert Bruce. Our

[1] *Select Biographies,* vol. i. p. 307.
[2] Wodrow's *Life of R. Boyd* (Maitland Club), p. 269.
[3] Hill Burton, vol. v. p. 271.

present interest centres in the unusually frank relations disclosed by the letters which the King wrote to his minister in Edinburgh.[1] His confidence in Bruce may be estimated when it is stated that the latter was chosen to act with the Council of State as a temporary government in the King's absence. Another proof of the royal favour was the fact that James, one week before he left Scotland, bestowed a gift for life upon Bruce out of the lands of the Abbey of Arbroath, amounting to twenty-five chalders of wheat.[2] In the King's letters Bruce is called Councillor, and his position was no sinecure, as is evident from references to his diligence both in James' own letters and in those written by Maitland, the Chancellor. Bruce was honoured with at least four letters from the King, some of them written in his own handwriting. "Good Master Robert, . . . I have heard of your daily travails now during my absence, as I think myself beholden while I live never to forget the same . . . For God's sake, take all the pains you can to tune our folks well now against our home-coming, lest we be all shamed before strangers, and exercise diligently your new office of redder and componer." He is anxious that three or four ships should be rigged up to do honour to the Queen on her arrival, and to escort the bridal party into Leith harbour. The letters are addressed to " our right trusty and well-beloved." In one of them he speaks jocularly to his correspondent of his Queen as " my new rib," and in another he bids him pray for a good wind to them; in a third letter the King thanks his devoted Councillor for the care he has given to the country in his absence, acknowledging that he is worthy of the quarter of his *petite* kingdom.

" The time has been," Bruce wrote years afterwards, when King James was his relentless enemy,—" the time has been that I have done his Majesty acceptable service, as his Highness' own handwriting beside me will bear record; which I shall leave to my posterity as their rarest jewels."[3]

The labours of Bruce during those six months in practical

[1] Wodrow's *Bruce*, pp. 17-21. [2] M'Crie's *Melville*, p. 230, n.
[3] Cald., vii. p. 183.

administration show that, had not the Church early claimed him, this man might have borne a conspicuous part in guiding affairs of State. It was admitted on all hands that the maintenance of order was largely due to him. " Of the favour of God," says James Melville devoutly, " there was never a more peaceable and quiet estate of the country than during that time of the King's absence."[1] For Bruce was not only a mystic and a saint; he was a practical man of affairs. Truly, it is the most formidable combination on earth, when a man who has a businesslike grasp of affairs believes all the while that he is engaged in doing the will of heaven. Surely his God gave wisdom and guidance to Bruce, while he laboured in the management of the nation's concerns. And the secret of his success was that, like all wise workmen, he served the King and country, not only by his activities, but also by his intercessions.

Maitland, the Chancellor, spent this winter abroad along with his master, the King; and his occasional correspondence with Bruce is no less complimentary to the latter than that of James. Maitland was, in the opinion of Lord Burleigh, the wisest man in Scotland. He sympathised with the Church party, and some years later he secured for them from Parliament an Act which they regarded as their Magna Charta. Maitland's letters to Bruce reveal an extraordinary energy on the part of the minister. He has been able to befriend the Chancellor's wife with advice and help, for which her absent husband is very grateful. Maitland was too experienced a statesman to imagine that Bruce could avoid making enemies in the conduct of his great administration. " I hear," writes he, " that a great part of the envy that was wont to lie upon me is transferred to you. I shall do what I can to haste me home, to sustain my part, lest you be overcharged."[2]

It must be confessed that the Scottish people, for all their reputed austerity, knew how to make their young Queen welcome to her capital. The pageant was all that the royal bridegroom could have desired. It was in the month of May that the ship which bore home this wedded pair cast anchor in the

[1] Melville's *Diary*, p. 277.   [2] Cald., v. pp. 85, 93.

port of Leith. The King conducted his bride towards Edinburgh by a prepared way, covered with tapestry and cloth of gold, "so that her feet did not touch the earth." Orations and sermons were addressed to the lady in Latin, French, English and Scots. Andrew Melville's Latin speech surpassed all the rest, and the King, who really knew Latin, acknowledged that he honoured him and his country that day, promising never to forget the obligation. As James passed into the Church of Leith, to give thanks for his prosperous return, Bruce came to him, and was received with a cordial embrace, the two men communing for a long time together. Surrounded by his nobles, James rode on horseback towards Holyrood, his Queen being driven in a coach and eight horses. Taking Queen Anne by the hand, James himself led her into the chambers of the ancient palace.

Two questions arose for settlement, which caused some delay. Might the coronation take place on Sunday? Was it proper to anoint with oil? Not for the first time was the latter question agitated, for upon the occasion of the crowning of James himself Knox had objected to the ceremony of anointing as being Romish.[1] The view of Knox would have weight with the ministers who were about to bear a part in the crowning of James' consort. The difficulty was a real one, and was only overcome when a declaration was set down in writing that the ceremony of anointing had no religious significance, but was merely a civil ceremony which a subject might lawfully perform at the King's command. Half a dozen of the chief ministers had been chosen to represent the Church at the coronation, and from among these it fell to Master Robert Bruce to anoint the Queen with oil. At length, on Sunday, 17th May, Anne of Denmark (she was but sixteen years of age at the time), was solemnly crowned Queen of Scotland in the Abbey Kirk. Maitland bore the crown matrimonial; two noble lords jointly placed it on her head. At this point it will be best to quote verbatim the old record: "The Countess of Mar opens the craig of her gown, and lays back a certain part of it. Master Robert

[1] Hill Burton, vol. iv. p. 284.

Bruce immediately pours forth upon those parts of her breast and arm which were exposed a bonnie quantity of oil "; whereupon a kerchief of white silk was wrapped round the shoulders of the Queen. " Her Majesty then retires, attended by her two virgins of Denmark, and having put on a princely robe, returns again to her own seat in the kirk. The King sends the sceptre which the said Master Robert delivered to Her Majesty, speaking these few words to her: We, by authority of the King's Majesty, with consent of his Estates, representing the whole body of the country, place this crown upon your Majesty's head and we deliver this sceptre unto your Highness, acknowledging you to be our Sovereign Queen and Lady; to whom we promise obedience, . . . and we crave from your Majesty the confession of the faith and religion which we profess." Bruce then made a " short narration " to the nobility and people of " the innumerable benefits bestowed by God upon this country, that first He had given them a King brought up sincerely in the true religion, and had given to him the Queen's Majesty, to be a helper, professing the same religion, to our great comfort."[1]

Afterwards Bruce preached in St. Giles before the King and Queen, tactfully limiting the service to half an hour. The impartial testimony of a foreign scholar who witnessed the entire pageant may be quoted. In a Latin poem which he wrote to celebrate the event he lauded Bruce for his part in the ceremonial: " A man of noble mien; among all that robed throng, second to none either in piety or in gifts." But what impressed this observer most was the prayer offered by Bruce, in which the minister commended the whole august proceedings to God, with holy vows,—" a man," the poet concludes " of wise disposition and learned in tongues."[2]

---

[1] *Coronation of the Queen's Majesty*, p. 53 (Bannatyne Club).
[2] M'Crie's *Melville*, p. 432. The poet's name was Damman.

CHAPTER VII

Conflicts between the Kirk and the King

THE year 1589 opened with many disquieting rumours concerning an imminent Catholic invasion. And unless we understand how serious were the grounds for alarm we cannot appreciate the bearing of the Reformers towards their antagonists. That a serious conspiracy was afoot is evident from a curious packet of letters which became public, causing the utmost alarm to the Church party.[1] They were intercepted in England, and, falling into the hands of Queen Elizabeth, were at once forwarded to King James. Their purport is to induce the Spanish King to attempt another invasion of the island. The active agents are certain Jesuits, but the occurrence of names like those of Huntly and Errol among the conspirators roused the alarm of every Protestant. Huntly, it transpires, had subscribed the Confession of Faith with a hand that was the while in correspondence with Philip of Spain. Errol was a correspondent of the minister, Master Robert Bruce, to whom he protested his loyalty to the Church,[2] while at the same time he maintained active intercourse with another Bruce, the Jesuit spy. It is necessary to point out carefully that about this time there were two of the name of Bruce resident in Edinburgh, who figure in these conflicts, and the danger of confusing them together is all the greater that they were both Robert Bruce, and both of them, it appears, were university graduates. The namesake of the Reverend Robert Bruce was no connection of the ancient House of Airth. He was a hired agent of the King of Spain. It is unfortunate that more than one student of the period has

[1] Thorpe's *Calendar of State Papers*, p. 554   Cald., v. pp. 6-34.
[2] Cald., v. p. 52.

attributed to the good minister certain actions of this other Robert Bruce. The author of the *Scots Worthies* has confused together the two men of the name of Robert Bruce; and Mr. Andrew Lang has not always succeeded in marking the distinction.

This other Robert Bruce is a different sort of person from the straightforward Presbyterian minister. He is a crafty Jesuit, dealing in an alias, changing sides with facility. There is a letter from him (August 1592) offering to betray the proposals of Spain to the English agent at the Court of James.[1] On the other hand, we find him busy, at the date to which the packet before us belongs, distributing Spanish gold,[2] and secretly arranging for the coming and the going of his fellow-conspirators by way of Port Seton, a quiet harbour near Edinburgh. In his letters all Scottish Presbyterians are heretics, and the Reformation is anathema. He is a man of education, writes in French, and he uses a careful cypher for the sake of secrecy. This packet of letters is but one sample of those " alarums " which periodically disturbed the peace of the kingdom, and brought home to the people the conviction that the Reformers were the patriotic party, and that a Catholic victory meant a victory for the enemies of Scotland.

Others besides the Earls of Errol and Huntly were involved in this treasonable correspondence: among them, the Lord Livingstone, designated by the Jesuit Bruce " a very Catholic lord." It will be remembered that this very Catholic Lord Livingstone was an uncle of Bruce the minister. Into his hands had been put a large sum of Spanish gold, and so soon as this fact came out in the Council a convoy was despatched to Lord Livingstone's home at Callander, with commission to search for the money. Some warning, however, must have been given, for the treasure had been removed, and the convoy returned with empty hands.

As a consequence of these rumours of impending invasion the city of Edinburgh was in a state of disturbance, the worthy

---

[1] *Calendar of State Papers, Scotland*, ii. 612.
[2] Thorpe, *Calendar, Scotland*, pp. 505, 640.

burgesses stood at arms, and the commission of the Church
met weekly for a time, in order to see to it (in their own classic
phrase), *Ne quid ecclesia detrimenti capiat*. It was felt that the
moment for firm action had come. All was at stake—the lives
of the people, the liberties of their country, freedom for public
worship; all that had been purchased at so great a price was in
danger of being snatched out of their grasp. Unless the Reformers would betray their heritage they must strike swift and
soon.

The characteristic policy of King James was to temporise,
and to balance the Protestant party against the Catholic. He
made a great show of taking severe measures against Huntly,
whom he imprisoned in the Castle of Edinburgh; but soon after,
the King did him the honour of dining with him in the castle,
" kissing him often, and protesting his belief in the earl's innocence." This might be " kingcraft," to use a favourite expression of James; but it was a line wholly obnoxious to the Reformers. And it was felt that his Majesty was properly served
when, shortly after, the two Catholic lords, Huntly and Errol,
were found in arms against him in the North. James was
forced to take the field against them in person, and their revolt
was soon quelled, its ringleaders being thrown into prison. As
for the Church leaders, one can well understand how rude a
shock was dealt to their faith in the word of their King, when
they saw these treacherous noblemen at large again before the
close of the year.

There was one striking episode, which occurred in the Great
Kirk of St. Giles on the occasion of thanksgiving for his
Majesty's prosperous return with his bride. On this day the
King stood up in the church and made a speech wherein, among
other assurances, he vowed amendment where he had fallen
short in matters that concerned the Kirk. At the Assembly of
the same year he promised that he would clear the land of
Jesuits, and he delivered a dramatic oration, wherein he praised
God that he was born in such a time, and that he was King in
such a Kirk, the sincerest Kirk in the world. " Stand to your
party," said his Majesty, " and I, so long as I brook my life

and crown, shall maintain the same against all enemies."[1] This may have been only kingcraft, but the speech so delighted the assembly that there was nothing save loud praising of God and praying for the King for a quarter of an hour.

The disappointment of these churchmen was extreme when gradually they discovered that the promises of James were a broken reed, and that he was cultivating the Catholic lords as far as he dared. Another ground of unsettlement in the minds of the people was the prevalence of disorder in the land, misrule and open vice breaking out in every direction among all classes. Bothwell, the madcap lord, boldly defied the law within the very capital, till King James was afraid to live in his own Palace of Holyrood.[2] How wretched must have been the condition of humbler folk when the King himself, under the very shadow of his castle, was in constant fear. Outrage and robbery were daily occurrences, murders went unpunished, there was no justice procurable in the land. It was rumoured that Captain Robert Bruce, the Jesuit spy, was in the neighbourhood, scattering lavishly his Spanish gold. It was at this critical point that the voice of St. Giles took a bolder note, and made itself heard to some purpose. Preaching in presence of his King, the minister, greatly daring, asked what the sore disobedience of the land could mean now while the King was present, seeing that some reverence was borne to his shadow when he was absent (in Norway). The preacher answered his own question. It meant a universal contempt on the part of his subjects. Therefore the King ought to call upon God before he either ate or drank, that the Lord would give him a resolution to execute justice upon malefactors, although it should be with the hazard of his life. If he would face this with courage the Lord would raise enough supporters, and every impediment would vanish. "Otherwise," said Bruce, "ye will not be suffered to brook your crown alone, but every man will have one."[3] These bold words were naturally resented, as was a reply which Bruce (according to Spottiswood) made in private

[1] Cald., v. p. 106.　　　　　[2] Ibid., v. p. 168.
[3] Ibid., v. p. 129.

when he talked with the King about the proposed restoration of Huntly: " Sir, if you take Huntly into favour, I will oppose; and you shall choose whether you will lose Huntly or me; for us both you cannot keep."[1] This saucy reply, as Spottiswood called it, incensed the King. Churchmen have been disposed to deny its authenticity, but it bears on it the stamp of verity; and it shows how acute the crisis had become between the contending factions.

The year 1592 was signalised by the tragical slaughter of the Earl of Moray, the same night that his house of Donibristle was burnt to the ground. The Earl of Huntly was the perpetrator of the crime, and the callousness of King James, as well as his evident desire to screen the murderer, roused the utmost popular indignation. The general feeling found its expression in a ballad, " The Bonnie Earl of Moray "—

> " He was a blaw callant,
>   And he played at the ba';
>   And the bonnie Earl of Moray
>   Was the flower among them a'."

The picture of Moray's streaming hair, all ablaze, by which the murderer was guided to his place of concealment, and his final words, when Huntly gashed his brow, " You have spoiled a better face than your own," are of the stuff that appeals to popular sentiment. It was impossible that the ministers should remain silent with reference to this outrage. The formidable weapon of excommunication was still in their hands, and they proceeded to place Huntly under this ban, which would entail social as well as religious ostracism. The King, upon this, burst into a rage, and threatened to break the heads of the ministers.

No one can in fairness charge Master Patrick Simson, minister of Stirling, with unbridled speech. The Scottish Church never contained a more gracious spirit in her ordained ministry. How greatly agitated the community had become can, then, be

---

[1] Spottiswood, *History*, bk. vi. p. 417. The story depends entirely on Spottiswood's authority.

C

judged if we consider the ominous words uttered by this gentle-mannered Scottish minister, a few days after the Donibristle murder, on the text, " Where is Abel thy brother?" The King was present, and the preacher addressed him as follows: " Sir, I assure you, in God's name, the Lord will ask at you where is the Earl of Moray, your brother." The King naturally resented this public rebuke, and spoke up before the congregation: " Master Patrick, my chamber-door was never closed to you; ye might have told me anything you thought in secret." The other replied: " Sir, the scandal is public." And after sermon, being sent for to the castle, he went up with his Bible under his arm, affirming that it would plead for him.[1] In comparison with Simson's language, that of Bruce, employed in a sermon which some time later he preached before the King, will appear moderate. The avengers of Moray's blood threatened his Majesty at his very palace gate. It is to this that Bruce refers, adding: " Your Majesty has had many admonitions, as we of the ministry and other estates have had; but this last admonition is sharper than the former, that now they pretend they come to seek justice for the last horrible murder." How, he asked, could the King punish others when he was pursued himself, and he bade him humble himself upon his knees and confess his negligence to God, and keep his promise better than he did the last which he made in that place. James retorted with great spirit, refusing to humble himself on his knees, and correcting the preacher in some of his details. He called upon all his men to thank God for the safety of his person, and to assist him in pursuing the traitors.

So unpopular did the King become in his own capital, after the affair of Donibristle, that he had to withdraw from the city for a while. The royal unpopularity served the Church, how-ever, in the end, for it resulted in the King, to please the Church and to regain a measure of her forfeited support, granting her what has been regarded as the very charter of her liberties. At an Assembly, held in Edinburgh, the honour of a second moderatorship fell to Bruce. To his influence was largely due

[1] Row, *Hist.*, p. 144.

the securing by the Church of guarantees for freedom to meet in General Assembly, for the purging out of heresy, and for the repeal of the Black Acts of 1584. By the advice of Sir John Maitland, the Chancellor, these demands of the Assembly were incorporated in an Act of Parliament, and received the royal sanction.[1] Maitland had shared in the unpopularity of James, and it was his subtle expectation, by conceding this measure to the Church, to recover both for his King and for himself the ground which had been lost. " God works," so runs the comment of James Melville,—" God works for the comfort of His Kirk by all kinds of instruments; to Whom, therefore, be all praise and thanks for ever."[2]

The Church, in this hour of her victory, appears to have embarked upon dictatorial courses, which raised up against her a new array of opponents. In the city of Edinburgh there was a body of people whose interest was neither Catholic nor Protestant. Indifferent as many of the craftsmen were to party conflicts, they were easily roused when their own interests were at stake. Now the clergy, in the plenitude of their power, desiring to secure a better observance of the Sabbath, ventured to make the drastic proposal that the day of holding the wool-market be altered from Monday to Wednesday.[3] Early preparations for marketing on the Monday had led to interference with the quiet of Sabbath evenings. One might as readily meddle with the rise and fall of tides as tamper with the incidence of a market-day, where (as in this case) old customs and financial interests barred the way. Other ecclesiastical interferences with their crafts, such as the prohibition of traffic with Spain till all fear of the Inquisition should be at an end, hastened a revolt on the part of the merchant class. It was indeed a case of interference with the rightful liberties of others by the very men who stood in Scotland for liberty, whether in Church or State. Rightly, the interference, however well meant, was resented. The craft of shoemakers were foremost in their demonstrations, surrounding the house of the ministers, and threatening to chase

---

[1] Cald., v. pp. 162-166.   [2] Melville's *Diary*, p. 298.
[3] Cald., v. pp. 177, 178, 188.

them out of the town. It was a characteristic of the period, much as we might hold a public meeting of protest, to give vent to strong, pent-up feelings in verse; and a lampoon which was flung in derision into the pulpit of St. Giles reveals their mental condition.[1] " Watson's words and Bruce's boast " will not avail to overawe the merchants. The Church has been " crying for more kirks," and the " collections " have been a grievous burden. The clergy are stigmatised, in short, " as wolves clad in wethers' weeds." One of the ministers declared that this mob of Edinburgh, when unrepentant and unbelieving, were more to be dreaded, for their antagonism to the Church, than the Court itself.[2] It can well be understood that these fresh anxieties of the ministers caused great merriment down at Holyrood. It was said at Court that " rascals and souters " had more power over ministers than the King himself had.[3]

A charge was brought this year against Bruce by two unscrupulous partisans, in the hope of destroying his influence. One of the two, Thomas Tyrie, was well known to be an agent of the Catholic party; the other, Patrick, Master of Grey, was a notable turncoat, a man of whom once great things had been expected by the Reformers; but, alas! he had more lately sunk into the commission of deeds of treason and forgery. The charge brought against Bruce by these miscreants was that of harbouring the rebel Bothwell in his house. Bothwell was the same man who, three years before, had knelt in St. Giles Church, feigning repentance and vowing a new life, the while he meditated on fresh crimes. Once on a time a habitué of Catholic circles, now he affected great zeal for the Protestant cause, and sought an alliance with the Church. Therefore, of course, it suited the opposite side to stigmatize the Church party, by this attempted setting of Bothwell in their company. The King gave ear to their accusations, and roundly charged the ministers that, while they denounced the Catholic earls as traitors, they shielded the firebrand Bothwell, who had lately made an attempt upon the life of his sovereign. Bruce was

[1] Cald., v. p. 177. [2] *Ibid.*, v. p. 338.
[3] Spottiswood, *History*, p. 394 (souters=shoemakers).

singled out specially, and charged with conspiring with others to put the crown upon Bothwell's head.

Now, if there was a loyal heart in Scotland, it was that of Robert Bruce. He could not lie or sell his soul for his King, but he prayed for him. He sought always for his salvation, both temporal and eternal. This charge of high treason was abhorrent to the leal-hearted minister, and he met it with a front of iron resolve and a stern demand for proofs. The King airily withdrew the charge, and requested that nothing more should be said on the matter. But he reckoned without his host. Bruce, in the manner of his time, brought the whole matter to the pulpit, declaring that he must abstain from preaching till he was cleared of the grave charge which had been levelled against him. Whatever might touch his honour, or might take from the weight of his ministry, Bruce was quick to resent. He desired to have a conscience void of offence, and a life purged from scandal. His bold front daunted the Master of Grey, who denied that he had made any accusations, and offered to fight anyone (his Majesty excepted) who should say otherwise. Whereupon Bruce marched down to Holyrood with his kirk-session behind him, and demanded to be confronted with his accusers. The King, who was never brave in face-to-face encounter, begged that the matter should be forgotten, and was annoyed at the determination of the minister. This incident was the beginning of an estrangement which was never afterwards healed.

It would be tedious to enter into further detail concerning those agitations in which Bruce took a leading part during the months which followed. Meetings were held in " Master Robert Bruce his gallery "; deputations were sent down to Holyrood; Courts of the Church met and gravely deliberated. There is no doubt that the Church party had a tender feeling towards that nobleman, Bothwell. Had he not professed penitence, and avowed his adhesion to the Cause?—might not this wild lord, with so great a pedigree, be turned and shapen into the appointed leader? Bruce, as their spokesman, declared roundly that Bothwell had taken up the defence of the good cause, at least the pretence thereof; to the King's shame, who took not upon himself the quarrel. The incident of Bothwell's forcing his way into the royal presence at midnight, and on his knees making terms with the King, should be read in Mr. Andrew Lang's picturesque description. The madcap earl held his Majesty as a sort of prisoner till he yielded. Edinburgh citizens must often in those days have held their sides with laughter over the grotesque figure of their King. He seemed unable to do things like other men. An element of the farcical runs through all his career, and in no instance more signally than in this.[1] Bruce took a leading part in the final arrangement of terms between Bothwell, the Church, and the King. A letter of the minister, written to some fellow-presbyters, may still be read, detailing this settlement. One can at least feel, as one reads the delicate adjustment of conditions, how heavy a burden of affairs, both public and ecclesiastical, rested on the shoulders of Bruce.[2]

[1] Mr. Andrew Lang's *History of Scotland*, vol. ii. pp. 371-373.
[2] Cald., v. p. 279.

CHAPTER VIII

The Sacrament of the Supper at St. Giles

In the Second Book of Discipline, approven by the General Assembly of 1578, the hand of Andrew Melville draws a distinction between the civil and the ecclesiastical power, such as it has always been the business of the Scottish Church to maintain. " Jesus Christ," the book declares, " has appointed a government in His Church distinct from civil government, which is to be exercised in His name by such officers as He has authorised, and not by civil magistrates or under their direction." The frontiers that divide these two sovereignties are clearly drawn : " Civil authority has for its direct and proper object the promoting of external peace and quietness among the subjects; ecclesiastical authority, the directing of men in matters of religion and which appertain to conscience. The former enforces obedience by external means, the latter by spiritual means." In the vindication of this great principle of the spiritual independence of the Church it has been the lot of the Scottish Church to suffer even from the days when Knox himself declared: " Take from us the freedom of Assemblies, and you take from us the evangel," to the latest Church crisis of the present century, when the matter in dispute was, " Whether Christ shall be Master in His own House."

Freedom of Assemblies, freedom to govern their Church and to direct her spiritual affairs, freedom from Erastian tyranny at the hands of the State; these were the main contendings of our forefathers in the Church of the later Reformation. King James' policy amounted to the substitution of the absolute control of the State for that of the Papacy, and the reduction of the Scottish Church to a mere department of his own administration. Those resolute Churchmen who were led by

Melville and Bruce had far too exalted a conception of what was due to their Spiritual Head tamely to submit to this indignity. It needs no argument to prove that the real Churchmen of the period we are considering were not the facile party of the Court, but those resolute Presbyterians with their high doctrine of *imperium in imperio*. Andrew Melville became the spokesman of this splendid claim, when he stood up before James VI. and said: "There are two Kings in Scotland, the one King James, the other Jesus Christ, of whose kingdom James is but a subject and a member." Is it impossible to vindicate this doctrine of spiritual independence? The Church has always been ready to contend for it by suffering, if not otherwise; and it must be admitted that she has paid an ungrudging price for the vindication of her sublime claim. And certainly, that thorough-going Erastian, Spottiswood, and his party, pliant instruments of the policy of King James, cut a poor figure in history compared with their stout antagonists.

Quite in accord with this doctrine of the Church is the doctrine of the sacraments held by the Scottish Presbyterians. In the Scottish Confession of 1560 it is taught that "In the Supper rychtlie used, Christ Iesus is so joyned with us that He becumis the verray nurishement and food of our saulis."[1] Master Robert Bruce, who was a theologian and a student of the history of the Church, bases his teaching upon the sacrament on this Confession, avoiding on the one side extreme sacramental ideas, and on the other side that lax teaching of the opponents of High Churchism which finds in the bread and wine no more than a picture of the transactions of Calvary. Bruce occupies the ground of the Second Helvetic Confession (1566) and of the Thirty-nine Articles (1563), which was afterwards defined in the Westminster Confession of Faith (1646). In his Five Sermons upon the Lord's Supper the view represented by that strong composition, the Scottish Confession of 1560, is laid down with

[1] The Scottish Confession is very forcible in its repudiation of the bald theory of commemoration: "Thairfoir whosoever sclandereth us, as that we affirmed or beleved sacramentis to be onlie naiked and bair signes, do injury unto us, and speak against a manifest treuth." —Laing's *Works of John Knox*, vol. ii. p. 115.

much vigour of intellect and variety of illustration. He steers a straight course between the Scylla of transubstantiation and what he regards as the Charybdis of a bare commemoration theory. In the words of his original, " We will neather wirschip the signes in place of that which is signifeid by thame; neather yit do we dispyse and interprete thame as unprofitable and vane; but we do use thame with all reverence, examyning our-selfis diligentlie befoir that so we do."[1] Or let Master Robert himself state the position : " Will ye speare at us, again, How Christ Iesus His true bodie and blood is present? We will say, That they are spirituallie present, reallie presente, that is present in the supper and not in the bread; we will not say that His true flesh is presente to the hande or to the mouth of our bodie, but we say it is spirituallie present, that is present to thy spirit and faithfull saull, yea even als present inwardlie to thy saul as the bread and wine are present to thy bodie outwardlie. Will ye speare then, Gif the bodie and blood of Christ Iesus be present in the supper? We answer in a word, They are present in the supper, but not in the bread and wine, nor in the accidents nor substance of bread and wine. And we make Christ to be present in the supper, because he is present to my saull, to my spirit and faith."[2]

It is quite essential, expounding the sacrament in a city lately delivered from Popery, to labour this point, so that again and again we come upon passages like the following: " To the end, therefore, that this sacrament may nurish thee to life everlasting, thou maun get in it thy hail Saviour, hail Christ, God and man, with His hail graces and benefits, without separation of His substance fra His graces, or of the ane nature fra the uther. And how get I Him? Not be my mouth. It is a vain thing to think that we will get God be our mouth. But we get Him be faith: as He is a Spirit, sa I eat Him be faith and beleif in my saul; not be the teeth of my mouth, that is a vain thing. I give thee, that thou might eat the flesh of Christ with thy teeth, and this were a cruel manner of doing; yit

---

[1] Laing's *Works of John Knox*, vol. ii. p. 115.
[2] Wodrow's *Bruce's Sermons*, p. 94.

thou may not eat the God-head with thy teeth: this is a grosse faschioun of speaking. Sa, gif ever ye get good of the sacrament, ye man get hail Christ; and there is not ane instrument to grippe Him, bot be faith onelie; therefore, come with a faithfull hart."[1]

"We get no more in the sacraments," says the preacher, "than we get in the word." "Quherefore are they annexed, seeing we gat na mair in the sacrament nor we get in the word; and we get als meekle in the very simple word as we gat in the sacrament? . . . It is true certainly we get na new thing in the sacrament, nor we get na uther thing in the sacrament nor we gat in the word, for quhat mair walde thou crave nor to get the Sonne of God, gif thou get him weill? . . ."

"Suppose thou get that same thing quhilk thou gat in the word, yit thou gets that same thing better. Quhat is that better? . . . we get Christ better nor we did before; we get the thing that we gat mair fullie, that is with a surer apprehension nor we had of before; we get a better grip of Christ now. For be the sacrament my faith is nurished, the bounds of my saul is enlarged, and sa quhere I had but a little grip of Christ before as it were betwixt my finger and my thumbe, now I get him in my haill hande; and aye the mair that my faith growes. the better grip I get of Christ Iesus. Sa the sacrament is felloun necessarie."[2]

The manner of the Lord's Supper, as set forth in the Book of Common Order, was simple and direct. This Book of Common Order prescribed no ritual, but offered guidance for the conduct of divine service. It was not permitted to receive the sacrament kneeling, nor to kneel in public prayers. The bread and the wine were dispensed by the minister and elders, being also passed from hand to hand by those who partook. It was enacted that in towns the communion be ministered

---

[1] Wodrow's *Bruce's Sermons*, p. 12.

[2] *Ibid.*, pp. 28, 49, 50. The old-world language, and archaic spelling are so curious, and express Bruce's thought with so much greater force than a translation, that they are preserved throughout the present chapter. With a little patience they can be interpreted.

four times in the year, or once a month, as might be thought expedient. After the exhortation the minister came down from the pulpit, and sat at the table, all who would partake taking their places likewise.

In his earlier years Bruce preached and administered the sacraments in the Great Church of St. Giles. Latterly he was limited to an annexe of the Great Kirk, commonly known as the Little Kirk. This building may have suited his voice, which was by no means a strong one, but the arrangement suited ill the multitude who hung upon his ministry. A request was lodged that the partition should be altered for the better accommodating of the worshippers, as well as for greater convenience in administering the Lord's Supper.[1] Upon a certain historic occasion a congregation of four hundred grown-up men were gathered in the Little Kirk, so that we can form some idea of the size of Bruce's congregation. The church was extended by demolishing the partition in the year 1600.[2]

We must make an attempt in this chapter to bring up to our minds the scene upon Communion Sabbath in St. Giles Church in the year 1590. In 1590 in St. Giles the communicants sat in successive relays at tables specially set apart for the purpose, which were covered with a fair white cloth. As many as twelve or even sixteen of these tables were provided, about one hundred people sitting at each one. Little tokens of metal were used, and these were handed to the officiating elder on his admitting to the table. The Session Records of St. Giles for 1590 show that not port wine but claret was used; the quantity consumed was astonishing. Dr. Cameron Lees is of opinion that this enormous consumpt was due to the people's joyous sense of their title to share in the cup, which had been restricted to the clergy in the Church of Rome.[3] We might have been astonished, had we looked into St. Giles, at the youth of some of the celebrants. The evidence tends to prove that the custom of coming at an early age to communion was common in the Reformation Church. Robert Blair, afterwards

---

[1] Cald., v. p. 739. [2] Ibid., vi. p. 27.
[3] Dr. Cameron Lees, Book on St. Giles, pp. 139, 380.

a great preacher in the Scottish Church, was admitted by his minister at twelve years of age, and John Livingstone mentions that he partook of the communion at the hands of Master Patrick Simson when he attended school in Stirling. "There came such a trembling upon me that all my body shook, yet thereafter the fear and the trembling departed, and I got some comfort and assurance."[1] James Melville partook of the sacrament at Montrose in his thirteenth year, "with great reverence." We might learn a lesson from that old custom of earlier partaking, to encourage our people at a more tender age, when the emotions are strong, to take the great step of sitting down at the Lord's Table.

So soon as all those who would share in the celebration were seated, the presiding minister took bread and gave thanks. After the thanksgiving he broke the bread and delivered it to the people, who distributed it among themselves; and likewise he gave the cup. During this time some suitable passage of Scripture was read, so that not only eyes and senses might be occupied with the bread and wine, which are called the visible word; but heart and mind might also be fixed fully on the contemplation of the Lord's death. After the Action, as it was called, there was thanksgiving, followed by the solemn singing of Psalm ciii., "My soul give laud," or some such Psalm; and so the "blessing" as the people rose to depart.

Master Robert Bruce is distinguished among all the ministers of this period as one who was exceptionally honoured in the administration of the sacrament. None of his colleagues had a more lofty conception of its place and its value in the Church. One recalls how this is the man whose ordination and whose right to administer the sacraments were challenged by his enemies. So that it seems as if God bestowed an exceptional distinction upon His servant, setting His seal in this wise upon his ordination, granting him a rich and ripe teaching on the sacraments. The story of his first dispensing the sacrament is told by one of his devoted followers, John Livingstone. Bruce's curious reluctance to submit to ordination, or to under-

[1] *Select Biographies*, i. p. 132.

take the full responsibility of his position, was overcome by a well-meant compulsion on the part of his brethren. Evidently they perceived that he was burdened by a morbid shrinking, which they set themselves to overcome. Accordingly, one of his fellow-presbyters induced Bruce to seat himself beside him at the sacred table, and after having served two or three successive tables, he left the church and sent some of the elders to Master Robert, to beg of him that he should undertake the duty of dispensing the sacrament at the rest of the tables, for otherwise the work must be left incomplete. Faced by the expectant congregation, many of the assembled elders calling upon him to proceed, Bruce characteristically accepted the situation, as in itself an ordination to the sacred office, and rose to dispense the Lord's Supper. All who were present felt that the rite was administered with unusual power. Ever afterwards Bruce looked upon that day as the day of his ordination to the holy ministry by the laying on of hands, and he stoutly refused thereafter to submit to any ceremony of ordination which should treat him as a probationer still; he considered that any such process would make void all his previous acts of ministerial administration.[1] This incident must belong to a very early date in the Edinburgh ministry of Bruce, for we find him administering the sacrament so early as 1589.

From the study of the sermons upon the sacrament of the Lord's Supper, one gains an admirable impression of their author, and every student of the Life of Bruce ought to study them if possible in the original braid Scots dialect in which they are delivered. They were first published in 1590, at the pressing request of the kirk-session of St. Giles. Bruce was unwilling to consent to their publication, for he was conscious of the rude and homely terms in which they were set out. But he consented, in the hope that poor and simple ones might find comfort and instruction from them. An edition, with eleven other sermons of the author included, was published

[1] Livingstone's "Memorable Characteristics," *Select Biographies,* i. p. 305.

in ordinary English at London, 1617, under the title *The Way to True Peace and Rest*. The edition of 1843, edited by Dr. William Cunningham, restores the sermons of Bruce to their original Scottish form of language. The sermons have been greatly appreciated both in England and Scotland. For those who can still take the trouble to study them in their homely Scottish garb, they afford a pith, a humour, and a pathos which no translation can recover.

There is here brought before us a virile intellect engaged in the effort to state the doctrine of the Reformed Church upon the sacraments, as distinguished on the one hand from the Roman and on the other from the Zwinglian position; that is, from the transubstantiation theory and from that of mere commemoration. All Bruce's powers of logic, his skill in definition, his lucidity, are brought to bear on the theme. Professor Laidlaw's testimony is that the doctrine of the Reformed Church has never been better stated. Perhaps the most strong and decided statement in the treatise is that in which Bruce speaks of the sanctification of the elements: " We acknowledge that the elements, be the vertue of this word are changed, not in their substance, not in their nature nor yit in their substantiall and naturall properties. But we grant that the elements are changed in ane qualitie quhilk they had of before, in sick sort that thir elements are tane fra the common use quhereunto they served of before, and be the institution of Christ they are applyed now to ane halie use. Look how far the haly use differs from the common use; there is als great difference betwixt the elements this day in the ' Action,' and the thing that they were yesterday; . . . this change proceeds *fra the will of Christ*, . . . for that thing is halie quhilk God calls haly, and that thing is prophane quhilk God calls prophane."[1]

These sermons are written in a trenchant style, and they bear every mark of having been taken down as spoken. The author deals in frequent repetitions: he is above all things desirous of being understood; he speaks contemptuously of the Sophists using an unknown language, " For except ye hear Christ in

[1] Wodrow's *Bruce's Sermons*, p. 78.

ane familiar and hamelie language, ye cannot understand, and except ye understand it is not possible to you to beleeve." It is particularly fine to observe how this man of high culture, well read in the schoolmen and in the books of law, as well as in Holy Scripture, quotes his texts in the dialect of his humble hearers, if only he may better gain their attention thereby: " Thou are thrumbled and thrusted be the multitudes, and yit thou spearis, quha hes twitched thee? " or " Quhat can twine me fra the love of God? "

He has many doctors of the schools and Fathers of the Church whom incidentally he quotes, and we can make quite a catalogue of the folios which would have been found in his library at the manse of St. Giles: Tertullian, Athanasius, Chrysostom, Polycarp, Augustine, Irenæus " that auld writer "; but specially Augustine; " I leave many of the doctors purposely, and take me only to Augustine." He quotes Latin poetry, and refers to Amandus Polanus on the slaughter of the magicians; but chiefly he depends on Scripture, which he claims to have studied more closely than any other book;[1] and indeed the sermons are a complete vindication of that claim. And it is in the last resort upon the will of his Lord and the authority of Christ as unfolded in Holy Scripture that he bases his doctrine of the sacrament, rather than upon the Church and her authority.

One has here a controversialist well instructed in the great question of the sacraments which had divided Western Christendom, and well taught in the history of his Church. The disputation at Poissy, the magical powers attributed to those five words, *Hoc est enim corpus meum,* transubstantiation and " that idolatrous doctrine of that dumb messe," " the awful claim to remit sin to the dead as to the living," all are in his view. Every point in the controversy with the Papists is known to him, and he puts his arguments with incisive power.

It may seem to us, as we turn over these yellow pages, that the controversies are dead and buried. It may be so, but as

[1] See Wodrow's *Life of Bruce*, p. 137.

we make our way over these ancient battlefields we gain the impression that this man is a great living captain in the fight. We perceive amid the antique terms and propositions a penetrating flavour of faith which dies not, but communicates itself to us over three hundred years.

One or two transcendent matters there are which absorb the preacher always: the terror of Popery, that superstition from which early in his life he had escaped;[1] the sense of the eternal world above and beyond him for which he lives and labours; Scotland, his loved country at his feet—Scotland distraught with factions, suffering, sinning; Scotland for whose sake he is willing to spend and be spent always. There is a personal note in these pages that moves us as we read. "Ye have experienced, as I myselfe have, in quhat estate the heart and mind is before the light enter: the mind is lyand drowned in blindness and the heart is hardened."[2] All his natural and acquired gifts he brings to the service of his Lord. He quotes from the law books as well as from the Word of God; and the illustration of a "seal" commends itself to him in the sense in which Scottish lawyers use the seal, appended to a charter. An "evidence" is with him a document which establishes a claim at law.[3]

The last two sermons of the five are valuable as a separate treatise on conscience, drawn up with a view to preparing his catechumens for the Lord's table. They reveal this minister in another light—as one versed in problems that have a broader bearing than those of the Papacy, questions concerning man and man's soul, sin and its putting away, doubt and faith, pardon and the pacifying of conscience; in the unravelling of which he shows himself a master. His own former "doubting and stammering" stand him in good stead, as he addresses himself to the resolving of the difficulties of other men.

"The bodie sall leave the saull, and the saull sall leave the

---

[1] Rome evidently observed the power of Bruce's sermons on the Sacrament as a reply was printed in Antwerp in 1593. The author, William Reynolds, may have known Bruce as they were both students at Louvain about 1572.

[2] Wodrow's *Bruce's Sermons*, p. 122.   [3] *Ibid.*, p. 71.

bodie, but the conscience sall never leave the saull; but look quherever the saull gais, to the same place sall the conscience repair, and looke in quhat estate thy conscience is quhen thou dies, in the same estate sall it meet thee in that great day. Sa that gif thy conscience was a burriour to thee in the time of thy death, gif thou gat it not pacified in the time of thy death, it sall be a burriour to torment thee in that general judgment."[1]

"Is not this ane matter more nor wonderful that ane and the self-same conscience sall serve to sa monie uses in ane saul as to be ane continuall observer and marker of thy actions, ane accuser, ten thousand witnessis, a judge and a burriour and tormentour to execute thy awin sentence against thyselfe? Sa that the Lord misters never to seek a member of court out of thy awin saule, to make out a lawfull proces against thee; but thou sall have all thir within thyselfe, to make out a full process against thyselfe! Take heed to this: for there is never a word of this that sall fall to the ground, bot either ye sall feill it to your weill or to your everlasting woe. And this secret and particular judgment that every ane of you carries about with you, bydis sa sure and sa fast within you, that doe quhat ye can, gif ye would imploy your haill traveillis to blot it out, thou sall never get it scraped out of thy saull."[2]

He declares that the all-seeing eye of God can "pearce through the very secret hirnes of conscience," and here is the counsel he offers for the restoration of a good conscience: —

"It is not possible that ye can baith keep a good conscience and serve the affections of your heart; and therefore, to keep peace and health in thy saull, thou man bid thy lustis good-night." "Quhen ye fall, delay not to rise, but run to the fountain of mercy, and seek grace in time. Run to prayer; run to the Kirk of God, quherever it be, quhether it be in the field or in the town. Run to Christ Iesus, and crave mercy at Him, that ye may have peace in your consciences."[3]

---

[1] Wodrow's *Bruce's Sermons*, p. 108 (burriour=tormentor).
[2] *Ibid.*, p. 106 (misters=needs).
[3] *Ibid.*, pp. 109, 113 (hirnes=corners).

CHAPTER IX

The Seventeenth of December 1596

IT was about this time that John Maitland, Lord Thirlstane, the Chancellor of the kingdom, was called to his account. This great statesman had unquestionably been guided in his public policy rather by motives of statecraft than by any high principles; but the Church could not forget that it was to him she owed the happy settlement of 1592, and she was grateful. In his last illness, as he lay at the point of death in his Castle in Thirlstane, Maitland sent for Master Robert Bruce. Along with two Melvilles Bruce hastened to his bedside, and a remarkable interview took place between them. He was penitent and full of regrets for his life, expressing a wish that he had built a hospital for the benefit of the poor, and crying often for mercy. One of his last laments was for the way in which he had treated John Knox. " We left him," says James Melville, " at a very good estate for the life to come."[1]

The year 1596 opened with great promise for the Church. The chroniclers of her story speak of the purity and the beauty which were exhibited within her borders. " The assemblies of the saints were never so glorious," cries Calderwood, with enthusiasm. The ministers were very busy, and it may be thought by many students of this period that they outstepped their office, meddling with matters which were hardly within their province. They constituted themselves a sort of police in the land, and no one—from the King on his throne and the Queen in her palace, down to the most wretched hag whom a superstitious age suspected of witchcraft—was beyond the reach of their censures. It was during this year that a small but weighty clerical deputation—Andrew Melville, Robert

[1] Spottiswood, p. 411; Cald., v. 382; Melville's *Diary*, p. 329.

Bruce, and John Davidson—made its way to Holyrood, to remonstrate with the Queen because of certain light, thoughtless criticisms which she had passed upon the ministers of the Church. They charged her Majesty, in addition, with spending her time in frivolity amongst her maids of honour. The good ministers were ready to become her teachers in the better way of life, but Anne of Denmark had a will of her own, and she refused the brethren audience. She was busy at a dance; and asked them to come on a more convenient day.[1]

It would be a mistake, however, to suppose that the effort at reformation was directed only towards the Court. Much the most remarkable movement of the year, for which Churchmen gave thanks, was the united cry to God on the part of the General Assembly, that He should heal the Church and the ministry of every offence, and vouchsafe revival. A most extraordinary paper was laid on the table of the Assembly, wherein the faults of clergy and people were written down by brethren of " sharpest and best insight," that occasion might be made for reformation. The sins of the rank and file of the Church are not spared—" The corruption of all estates within this land," and offences are specified in the courts of justice and in the royal house. These are, however, touched upon but lightly in comparison with the faults of the ministry, upon which the compilers of this Assembly paper lay chief emphasis. Neglect of their book and of Scripture study, neglect of prayer and of attention to the sick, are specified; and also deeds of a more glaring sort. The Church surely needed purifying if a paragraph like the following could be unanimously agreed to in the great court of Assembly: " That ministers being found swearers, profaners of the Sabbath, drunkards, fighters, liars, flatterers, brawlers, be deposed. That ministers given to unlawful occupations for gain, as holding of hostelries, taking of usury (besides good conscience and laws), bearing worldly offices in noble and gentlemen's houses, merchandice and suchlike, buying of victual and keeping to dearth, be admonished: if they continue therein, be deposed."

[1] Cald., v. p 460.

" That ministers," this interesting paper concludes, " in all companies strive to be spiritual and profitable, and to talk of things pertaining to godliness, such as may strengthen them in Christ, and instruct in their calling."[1]

The acknowledgment of these gross abuses in public Assembly was followed by a wonderful Act of united humiliation on the part of the brethren. This was done upon no sudden impulse, but with deliberation. Many trusty religious guides there were, who stood up and exhorted the house. Patrick Simson, of Stirling; Robert Rollock, the Principal of Edinburgh University; Robert Bruce, minister of St. Giles, were present, as well as Andrew Melville. But the man who was divinely impelled to lead this new movement was a quiet minister from Prestonpans, John Davidson by name. Of great piety, of transparent honesty of purpose, one also whose culture commanded the respect of the house, he found himself, greatly against his will, summoned to preside at the diet set apart for the proposed solemn religious exercise. It was on a Friday that the Assembly commanded Davidson to undertake this office. He had to ride out to his own parish for Sunday duty, but on the following Tuesday, the day assigned, he was punctual at his post. Four hundred men gathered on the morning of that memorable day in Master Robert Bruce's kirk, all of them ministers or " choice professors." No others were admitted. After the opening prayer, and the Scripture lesson, which a reader recited from Ezekiel xxxiii. and xxxiv. (about lying prophets and shepherds that feed not the flock), Davidson rose and in choice words of much tenderness he invited his brethren to repent. By and by, as the reverend father waxed warm in his sermon, a sudden gust of emotion swept over his audience, and the kirk resounded with their sobbing.[2] It is no trifling occasion when strong men, proud nobles, reserved

---

[1] Melville's *Diary*, pp. 347-350.

[2] " He was so assisted by the Spirit working upon their hearts, that within an hour after they had convened, they began to look with another countenance than at first, and while he was exhorting them to these duties, the whole meeting was in tears.—Carslaw's edition of *The Scots Worthies*, p. 85.

Scotsmen can weep. Nothing like this had been known since the blessed Reformation of Knox, half a century previous. Davidson recognised the uniqueness of his opportunity, and, sitting down, he bade the brethren turn a while to private meditation and confession. For fifteen minutes the teacher and his scholars made such a lamentation that the kirk resounded, and the historian calls it Bochim, the place of weeping. The presiding minister, after further prayer, turned the thought of his hearers to the parable of the faithful and wise steward whom the Lord found watching, (Luke xii.), and so irresistible was the authority of God's word, that the entire assembly seemed to be stirred to its foundations. At the end of three hours, as they separated, the brethren banded themselves, with hands lifted up to heaven, in a new league of fidelity to God. This resolution was borne by zealous representatives into the local synods and presbyteries, so that the movement might be spread throughout the land.[1]

Such a striking episode deserves the detailed narrative given above, for the reader is led to think, owing to the preponderance of ecclesiastical and political affairs in the page of history, that Scotland in the seventeenth century was interested in little else. Unquestionably there was a profound religious revival afoot, and behind the strivings of parties there was operative a great spiritual work such as cannot be recorded in the bald narrative of history. Hints of this movement there are in abundance, upon which we shall light as we proceed.

Meantime the camp of the Protestants was shaken by rumours of the boldness of their opponents. The King entertained Papists at his palace. The Queen gave fresh umbrage to the Church at the baptism of her daughter. On the other hand his Majesty had a new ground of offence against his minister, Bruce, because of the escort of admirers who had attended the latter during a visitation of churches in the West Country. The royal rage was such that James vowed he should want Bruce's head, and he accused him anew of treason. While the Church party were anxiously opposing the return of

[1] Melville's *Diary*, p. 352; Cald., v. p. 406.

the Catholic noblemen to Scotland, King James instituted a
process against Master David Black, or Blake,[1] minister of
St. Andrews, for certain over-bold utterances made in a sermon. Bruce signalised himself by his doughty defence of
his brother minister, and the result was, of course, that his
relations with the Court were further strained.

Upon all this ensued the 17th of December, a day of melancholy omen to the Church, and a date which James VI
attempted to mark out as afterwards he marked the 5th of
November, the day of the Gunpowder Plot. But the riot of
17th December was really a small affair apart from the crafty
uses to which King James turned it, in his desire to prejudice
the Kirk. On the date in question a meeting of the Church
Council was convened as usual, noblemen and gentlemen
gathering in the Little Kirk, along with the ministers, the latter
being arrayed in their black gowns. Many versions of what
took place were circulated. The credible, authentic version
is that of Bruce himself, who was a central figure, and the
windows of whose house overlooked the street where the unfortunate tumult occurred. Most truthful of human beings,
Bruce supplies what he calls " the true history of all that which
passed among us that forenoon." " I speak the truth: I lie
not," says he, and no one who is familiar with his character
can doubt this testimony.

The menace of those " apostate lords," men who had been
trafficking with Italy and Spain, and who were about to return
to Scotland, lay like a nightmare on the Protestant gentlemen.
Lord Lindsay with three other laymen was sent to interview
the King; Master Robert Bruce was desired to go with them.
They found his Majesty at the Tolbooth, and he gave them but
an ill welcome, so that they had to return to the crowded
chapel of St. Giles. Ere the convocation broke up, they made
a fresh covenant to defend the good cause to the last breath.
Their noisy applause over this resolution brought Bruce to his
feet, that he might entreat the meeting to be quite and orderly
for the sake of the cause which they had all at heart. It was

[1] He is called Master David Blake in Spottiswood, p. 419, etc.

a necessary warning. The electric condition of the city is shown by the rapid gathering together of "the mean people," who were perhaps instigated by designing partisans, with a view to creating a prejudice against the Church. Some voice raised a shout: "A tumult! Arm! Arm!" Bruce all the while remained within the kirk or the kirkyard, which in those days surrounded St. Giles. A cry was raised that the ministers were slain, but the barons and others who were present hurried Master Robert for safety into his manse, which stood just across the narrow street. The street meantime was thronged with a noisy mob, the great part knowing not wherefore they were come together. Magistrates and ministers in combination at length succeeded in quieting it, and the ministers sent some of their number to Holyrood, with instructions to express their sore grief to the King on account of the tumult, and to beseech of him a remedy of their grievances. His Majesty was at this point most gracious, and his reply led to the dispersing of the Assemblage, who had come together for later conference, not inside the church but in the kirkyard. "We dissolved with a singular contentment, giving public thanks to our God, who by His providence had so well disposed of all things that day."[1]

As for the tumult itself, a "no popery" riot, as it has been called, they who convened in the Little Kirk that day were so far from being its cause that they were the means of quelling it. "I had rather have been banished my country for ever," wrote Bruce, "ere one drop of blood had been shed that day." "And I am heartily sorry that our holy and gracious cause should be obscured by the tumult." "Surely before Huntly came home I am of opinion that no man of my calling was further in his Majesty's affections than I; and I am persuaded that if the Papists had not returned towards us, I had continued so. I might also report me to her Majesty. She can testify what was my care and solicitude for him."

By and by a garbled account of the origin of the tumult was brought to the King, with the result that he changed his mind, flew into a rage with the ministers of the Church,

[1] Bruce's "Apology," Cald., v. p. 563. *Ibid.*, p. 568.

ordered the immediate arrest of certain citizens who were impli-
cated in the tumult, and withdrew his Court from the capital
to Linlithgow. Bruce and the other ministers of Edinburgh,
deeming discretion the better part of valour, fled from the city
till the royal wrath should be assuaged. Bruce and a friend
escaped into Yorkshire, and there was neither preaching nor
prayer heard in the kirks of Edinburgh for a great space.[1]
Bruce and his friends deemed it necessary to submit an explanation of their flight. " I am no deserter of the flock," writes
the minister of the Little Kirk; and he speaks of the tran-
quillity which God granted his spirit in his exile. " The hearts
of strangers were mollified, and all things made facile for our
convoy." He expresses his doubts that the persecutor would
ever return to a sounder mind. " Nam neque imperium, neque
philosophia mutat affectus, sed Spiritus Domini renovans."[2]
" And if the Lord should call us to suffer death for His truth,
should we not suffer? If He call us to banishment, wherein
oftentimes are more evils than death, let us embrace it also."
In the eloquent epistle which he addressed to the ministry
and to the city in vindication of himself and his brethren,
" From the mountain of the Lord's Providence, who is our
only hiding-place at this hour," there are allusions which reveal
the pastor's consuming anxiety over the state of the country.
Quoting Jeremiah, he looked longingly to a cottage of the
wilderness, where he might remain, never to return to the
land, to behold either the present enormities or the calamities
to come. But he has heard the cry of the daughter of Zion,
and beholds her bloody wounds, and he must stoop down to
her help. " Let us strive in prayer to bring ourselves to a
taste of a groaning and broken spirit. Let us fetch our sighs
from the very depth and bottom of our souls, and let us practise those Christian virtues which we have been preaching to
others, to wit, repentance, faith, hope, love, patience, sanctification, whereby we may glorify our God, edify our flocks,

[1] Moysie's *Memoirs* (Maitland Club).
[2] For neither rule (i.e. the power to rule) nor philosophy is able to
change the disposition; but (only) the regenerating Spirit of the Lord.

give good example to strangers, and keep joy in our own souls, with assurance that we shall see His face in glory. Pray for us, brethren, in spirit, that we make Christ our joy, our gain, our glory, as there is none able to fill our heart, and satisfy our affection in these three but He. To Him be praise, glory, and dominion, for ever and ever."[1]

The day after the tumult Master Robert Bruce, at the request of those nobles and others who acted with him in the emergency, wrote a letter to Lord Hamilton (a nobleman nearly related to the Royal House and of the blood royal), in which he mentioned the unhappy affair of 17th December, and stated that by God's grace the pastors had pacified the people. His purpose in writing was to invite his lordship as a great nobleman to come and countenance the Church in its difficulty, and especially to withstand those councillors who were moving the King against the ministry. A garbled copy of this letter was placed by Hamilton in King James' hands, by the reading of which his Majesty's anger against the Church was kindled to a fiercer heat. In the falsified edition of Bruce's letter the rioters are described as having been " animated no doubt by the word and motion of God's Spirit," and the claim of the ministers that they had repressed the tumult is left out altogether, the total effect being to convey the suggestion that Bruce sought Hamilton's aid to overthrow King James, a construction which the minister repudiated with indignation.

What Bruce keenly foresaw was in due course accomplished. King James turned this affair of 17th December to the securing of his own ends with the Church. He was astute enough to see that the tumult could be turned to the disadvantage of the ministers. Before this date he had been busily engaged in devising a scheme for the advancement of prelacy, and in the ensuing Assembly he found that he could command a majority of votes. This result was the more easily obtained because the Assembly met in the city of Perth, where a larger number of northern ministers convened than could be gathered in Edinburgh. By the votes of these men of Aberdeenshire and

[1] Cald., v. pp. 556-560.

the Highlands the voice of Fife and the Lothians was overcome.

The King re-entered his capital on New Year's Day 1597,
amid the ringing of bells and blowing of trumpets. The citizens
had been dismayed at the suggestion of the removal of the
Court from their midst, and they received their King again with
jubilation. In order to celebrate the event with proper dramatic
effect, the magistrates made him a banquet at Master Robert
Bruce's house.[1] It is probable that this house was the same
which Knox inhabited, 1560-66. It stood in Warriston's Close,
anciently Bruce's Close, and a brass has been set in the wall
by pious hands to testify, " near this spot stood the manse."
Curiously, there is a stone lintel set over the door of Chambers'
House in the same close, which bears the Kennet arms, and
the words, " Gratia Dei Robertus Bruiss." Though this
last is the name of another of the great family of Bruce, it
marks very nearly the spot where the minister dwelt; and
along with him in the same house there dwelt his colleagues
of St. Giles. It must have been a splendid building, that it
could be shared by all the ministers; and that it was suited
for a royal banquet. One condition laid down by the returned
victorious King was that the ministers must not live together
as they had done " in the circuit of a close."[2] Another condition was that Assemblies of the Church must not be held in
Edinburgh. A third was that the King should have power
to make ministers preach or desist as he thought fit, and that
he should have a voice in the filling of vacant churches. "So,"
says Calderwood, with reference to the banquet in the deserted
manse, " the King in a manner would triumph over the poor,
banished ministers."

A week after the banquet the four fugitive ministers were
allowed to re-enter the city of Edinburgh, and they gained
access to the royal presence. There were explanations, and
James was graciously pleased to approve of their action in
having taken to flight; " for," said he, " I might have done that

[1] Cald., v. p. 625.
[2] A. Lang, History of Scotland, vol. ii. p. 422.

in my anger which I would have regretted." His Majesty, says Calderwood, knew very well that they were innocent of any thought of treason. There were no more loyal men within the kingdom, even if their methods of exhibiting their loyalty did not always meet the approval of their royal master. Each one of the four made a declaration of loyalty, but the King held out long ere he consented to their restoration to the exercise of their ministry. It was the 24th of July ere they got leave to preach. "Certainly, sir," said Bruce, when he gained audience at Holyrood, "if I could have foreseen, or any way foreknown the consequences of the action which we had in hand that day, I would not for all the earth have entered on it. But as for these consequences, they were merely accidental, and grieved me as much as anything that ever fell out in my times in Edinburgh. Sir, since ye have begun so well, I pray your Majesty continue, and let me recover the room I was wont to have in your Majesty's affection. For my part, I will promise to serve you, and to study by all means your safety." He vowed to his King all due reverence, and added: "I know your calling is high and your person great, and craveth due reverence from all your subjects."

The King answered: "Surely, Master Robert, ye shall recover your room which ye had in my affections." After some short conference, the King said he would give him both heart and hand, and a reconciliation was for the time effected.[1]

[1] Cald., v. p. 653.

CHAPTER X

Domestic and Pastoral Life of Master Robert Bruce

THROUGH the din of public controversy those gentler voices are largely silenced by means of which there ought to be handed down the really interesting and inward history of a nation. The same holds good with regard to individual careers. It is not easy to reach the record of their true life. Bruce's own narrative is but a fragment, so far as it has yet been discovered, but it will be necessary for the biographer to investigate, with what material is left to his hand, those chapters of Master Robert's domestic and pastoral work which after all reveal the character of the man more than the strife of Church Courts, or than the combats in which he engaged with his sovereign.

The story of Bruce's family relations, if it is unfortunately brief, is very suggestive and creditable to him in every respect. It will be remembered that the cost of his fidelity to his conscience was his disinheriting about the year 1583. One is gratified to have to record that a few years later, on the occasion of the minister's marriage with Martha Douglas, the estate of Kinnaird was restored to him by the act of a father who with all his faults was generous-hearted in the extreme. We can still handle the title-deed which made over the property anew to "Master Robert Bruce, minister of God's word." Kinnaird is a beautifully situated and fertile property, near Larbert. A good view of the battlements of Airth Castle is obtained from the spot where Bruce's house stood. A century and a half later than the Reformer's day his descendant, James Bruce, the traveller, repaired and added to Kinnaird House. It was razed to the ground in 1897, and all that can be said of the present handsome house is that it marks the spot where the minister resided three hundred years ago.

Of the lady who became Bruce's wife little is known. She was no combatant in the fray like Mrs. Welsh, John Knox's daughter. But she must have had a practical turn : we find her brother-in-law writing to her on his father's death upon the temporal affairs of the family; and when her husband was forced to flee to France he made a deed assigning the charge of his affairs to his beloved spouse, Martha Douglas. Her grandfather, Douglas of Parkhead, was a fierce and determined Reformer; it was he who slew James Stewart, Earl of Arran, the arch-enemy of the Presbyterian cause. But Mrs. Robert Bruce was a gentle lady, whose sway was felt in the house more than outside. She suffered gladly alongside her husband, and faced the hardships of exile in his company. On the occasion of his second banishment to Inverness Martha Douglas was dead. Several touching letters and many references to her and to the children occur in Master Robert's correspondence. These prove her a true yoke-fellow, a sharer in the plans and in the anxieties of her husband. The betrothal ring of Robert Bruce and Martha Douglas is to this day in the hands of the representative of the family.[1]

There were two sons of the marriage, Robert and John. Of these the elder was attached to the Court, and followed his King into England. It was through the influence of this son, Robert, that leave was granted to the persecuted father to return to his own house of Kinnaird in 1613. To him the minister surrendered all his lands in 1623, on the occasion of the young man's marriage. John, the other son, became, like the sons of Knox, a clergyman of the Church of England. Of the two daughters, the elder, Elizabeth, married a north country laird in 1624. Martha, the younger, interests us more, for it was she who read the Bible to her father on his deathbed, and ministered to him. She must have been a mere girl on that occasion, for her marriage took place seventeen years after.

[1] M. E. Cumming Bruce, *Family Records of the Bruces* (Blackwood, 1870).

On the side of his mother, who opposed bitterly the decision of her illustrious son to enter the Christian ministry, it seems clear that cordial and even affectionate relations were ultimately restored. It is certain that Master Robert took up the rôle of counsellor and guide in the Airth family, as would naturally be expected from one of his high character and clerkly profession. He bore the reputation of a peacemaker, and among his papers is a scroll of a letter prepared for his mother, to attempt the ending of a dispute with some neighbour. There is also a very luminous letter, dated Airth, 25th August 1600, from his brother, Sir John Bruce of Kincavel. Many troubles had lately beset the house of Airth. Sir Alexander, the old laird, was just dead. The eldest brother had predeceased his father, and this third brother, John, writes begging that the minister should come to the castle to aid in settling family affairs. Nor did the good man forget Master Robert's own troubles. The Gowrie affair was uppermost that month in every mind, and its consequences for Master Robert were profound. His quarrel with the King appeared now to be hopeless. So we have a striking picture of the laird of Kincavel, Sir John, busy with his harvest, yet laying down the reaping-hook and taking up the pen to administer comfort to his sore-driven brother. After referring to " the piece of a cross wherewith it has pleased God to visit you now," the writer goes on : " This will not trouble you, nor put you much about, both in respect that it is His inestimable dealing towards you, and that you are better prepared, and can receive these visitations in better part than common men." His brother has little hope that the minister's tribulations will mend. " I look," he says, " that this shall be but a preparation for a greater, for the Lord deals with you as the good doctor of medicine does with his patients, who begins gently and softly on purpose to prepare the person for the bitter and sour medicine to come. So I think ye shall do well to provide for the worst, and the Lord grant you the assistance of His Spirit to that effect." This letter is addressed to " The Right Honourable his loving brother, Master Robert Bruce, minister of Christ's Evangel at

Edinburgh."[1] We shall meet the good laird, Bruce's correspondent, again, when he gives very practical aid to the persecuted preacher. It should be added as a notable proof of the trust reposed in Master Robert's uprightness by his own family that, when the eldest brother died, the minister was appointed guardian to the children, who were yet under age.

The minutes of Assembly of the Church of Scotland disclose during those years from 1586 to the end of the century, when Bruce was still a minister in active service at St. Giles, quite an amazing energy on his part in the affairs of the Church. His name figures upon every important committee, usually standing first, as became his rank. His hand is traceable in the drawing up of minutes, resolutions, protests. He is deputed to visit, east and west. In the west country his visitation of churches was such a popular triumph that the King was jealous, and vowed he would have Bruce's head.[2] The Assembly sent the minister to St. Andrews Presbytery in 1593 to settle matters of dispute in the kirk of that city.[3] We come upon Bruce's name in the minutes of Edinburgh Presbytery, taking a part in the settlement of Henry Blyth over the Canongate Church.

Master Robert was in much demand also as a pastor skilled in dealing with the spiritual needs of men. Whether it be in the Court of Holyrood, to remonstrate with Queen Anne for her follies, or in the closes of the High Street where his congregation dwelt, or in the prison of Edinburgh to minister to a condemned murderer, this servant of God enters ever with firm step and faithful message. Bold as John Knox himself in the face of kings, he is tender also, and rich in words of consolation. He is the sort of friend upon whom others can lean in the day of their trouble, as Christian leant upon Hopeful's shoulders when in the waters of Death. See him galloping down with two friends to the old Castle of Thirlstane at Lauder, where John Maitland the chancellor lay dying. Or follow him to the manse of Stirling, where aged Patrick Sim-

[1] *Bruces of Airth and their Cadets*, Armstrong, p. cii.
[2] Cald., v. p. 437.   [3] *Booke of Universall Kirk*, p. 390.

son lay in his last extremity.[1] What would we not thankfully give for a report of the last interview of these two men of God, Bruce and Simson?

Devoted admirers of Bruce will search in vain for any trace of those dwelling-houses and closes which knew his gracious presence in the end of the sixteenth century or at the beginning of the seventeenth. One wishes that it were possible to have fifteen minutes' conversation about the godly minister with men who knew him, such as John Howison in the West Port;[2] or Andrew Hart, the printer; or George Heriot, senior, the goldsmith, staunch friend of the minister, in whose mansion Bruce was always a welcome guest; or Alexander Merson, whose house Bruce visited in connection with his son's marriage.[3] Andrew Ainslie was another citizen who sheltered Bruce, and it is in his house that we find the old minister conferring with John Livingstone and the Tutor of Bonnington.[4] But most of all, one would wish to be able to recall Bruce's visits to the house of Mistress Rachel Arnot, of the Sciennes, that lady of the Covenants who sheltered the prophet when, like his Master, he had nowhere to lay his head. In her house Bruce seems to have for some years found a haven. She was a very rich woman, wife of Johnstoun, who is described as the greatest merchant of his time.[5] This locality, called the Sciennes from the fact that a convent dedicated to St. Catherine of Sienna stood there, was, in the day of the Reformers, half a mile distant from the city wall, and would afford a safe asylum for hunted men. It was probably here, in the house of good Rachel Arnot, that the ministers gathered to those meetings which are repeatedly referred to as taking place in the Sciennes. Kirkton, for example, refers to a great tryst of the Presbyterians which took place in the Sciennes, in the year 1621. Having been ordered to depart from Edinburgh, because they refused to observe the Five Articles of Perth,

---

[1] *Select Biographies,* vol. i. p. 106.   [2] Cald., vi. p. 196.
[3] Bruce's Narrative, Wodrow MS., folio 42; 42, Advocates' Library.
[4] J. Livingstone, "Memorable Characteristics," *Select Biographies,* vol. i. p. 307.
[5] Burnet's *History of His own Times,* vol. i., Oxford Ed., p. 25.

these ministers met, and spent in prayer and fasting the day upon which the objectionable Articles were to be ratified by Parliament—the Black Parliament it was called by them. The "faithful, aged ministers" prayed first, and got not access. Whereupon, at the suggestion of Lady Culross, David Dickson, a younger man, was called on to lead the devotions, which he did with much power, so as to strengthen the faith of all who were present.[1]

The effect of all this upon Rachel Arnot of the Sciennes is traceable in later days. She had no inconsiderable influence upon the ecclesiastical policy of the Church. And it was she who, with her daughter, Janet Johnstoun, prevailed on Sir James Skene (husband of the younger lady) to abstain from participating in the sacrament on account of its being administered to the partakers on their knees, by order of the Black Parliament.[2]

References like these are suggestive of a busy life within the city and about it. The magistrates had a great reverence for their minister, and we hear of their going out to Kinnaird House in a body to petition him to resume his office among them. It was at the house of one of them that Robert Bruce and John Davidson, minister of Prestonpans, met at dinner. The latter had some reputation as a prophet, and on rising from the table created consternation by announcing, with reference to their host, that he who showed the servants of God honour would in a short time carry them both to prison; which prophecy, it was averred, came shortly after to pass.[3]

These two, Bruce and Davidson, met another day at dinner during the period when Bruce was yet a favourite at the Court. This was the day on which the minister of Prestonpans sur-

---

[1] Bruce is not specially mentioned as present on this occasion, but he was at liberty that year, and was probably one of "the faithful aged ministers." See Preface to Warriston's *Diary*, Pub. Scot. Hist. Society; *Select Biographies*, vol. i. p. 317; Kirkton's *History*, pp. 16, 17, 18.

[2] Cald., vii. p. 383. One daughter of Rachel Arnot married a Bruce, of Stenhouse; of another of her children was descended Bishop Burnet the historian.

[3] Row, *Coronis*, p. 420.

D

prised the guests by referring to Bruce in his grace after meat as follows: "Lord, Thy servant here shall be within a little as much persecuted as he is now in favour; and go down the streets when many who have him this day in esteem will not give him a salutation." An extraordinary "grace," and very suggestive as to the plight in which Bruce found himself in Edinburgh on losing the royal favour.[1]

The sermons of Bruce show in a score of places that he had a deep interest in the suffering of the poor, and that he was their helper. We must picture him moving about amongst the closes and back wynds of his great charge, to exhort and to console, in fulfilment of his Master's words: "I was an hungred and ye gave me meat, sick and in prison and ye visited me." In the will of a Countess of Eglinton, dated 1596, occurs the following instructive clause: "I leave to the poor of Edinburgh, Leith and the Canongate, ijc merks, to be distributed to them by Master Robert Bruce, minister."[2] High and low, rich and poor, relied on Bruce's probity and sagacity.

There is one piteous tale of the period, which from its connection with Bruce must be related. It is one of the last episodes in the city of Edinburgh with which the minister was permitted to take to do ere he finally suffered banishment. The story is a luminous illustration of the life and doings of the seventeenth century.

Jean Livingstone was a beautiful young girl, belonging to a family which was connected by marriage with that of Airth, and her home at Dunipace was but two miles and a half from Master Robert's residence of Kinnaird. Jean had little guidance or affection in her own home, and she was married at the tender age of seventeen to the laird of Warriston, a man who proved a tyrant and a brute. Our modern taste will not allow

---

[1] Davidson had a reputation for compiling forms of prayer. His Presbytery (Haddington) bade him draw up a series of daily prayers as well as blessings for meals, to be used by the unlearned. Here is Davidson's form of grace before meat: "Blis us, guid Lord, and ther thi creatures, quhilk thé prepairest for our norishment. through Jesus Christ our Lord. Amen."—*Miscellany of Wodrow Society*, i. p. 540.

[2] *Memorials of the Montgomeries*, ii. p. 235.

of the recital of all the wrongs which at length goaded Jean Livingstone to the commission of her crime. The trial is given in detail in Pitcairn's *Criminal Trials*.[1] The man must have been demented, for he bit his wife and he flung a dish from the dinner-table at her face, cutting her cheek. At length, with the aid of two devoted adherents, she strangled the monster. There is a ballad, "The Laird of Warriston," in which the popular sympathy with Jean obtained its expression—

> "She's gimp about the middle
> As ony willy wand."

Both her father and her mother threw her over, the former refusing to see her or to intercede for her when she lay under sentence of death. Their family pride quenched in their breasts all natural affection—

> "Up spak the laird of Dunipace,
> Sat at the king's right knee,—
> 'Gar nail her in a tar-barrel,
> And hurl her in the sea.'"

Others there were, however, who pitied her, and the sentence was modified to one of beheading. During the three days of grace which lay between the sentence and the carrying of it out, Lady Warriston lay in prison at the Tolbooth, and there is a tract which one can still read. "*The great work of mercy which God wrought in the conversion of Jean Livingstone.*"[2] It is believed to be the work of that good minister, James Balfour, who was Bruce's colleague, and it gives with microscopic detail the incidents of those last days. "She was but a woman and a bairn," says the writer, and he so dealt with her that by the mercy of God she repented and found peace. "I desired her," says the author, "to send for Master Robert Bruce, that by his conference with her she might yet be

[1] Pitcairn's *Criminal Trials,* ii. p. 446.
[2] "Jean Kincaid, of Warriston: A Memorial of her Conversion, 1827. Ed. C. K. Sharpe."

further comforted and confirmed in her resolution. He came to her, and can bear witness of the working of God's gracious Spirit, which he saw in that woman, and of the wonderful contentment which she had in her God. So that servant of God, seeing and hearing such a merciful presence of God's Spirit in her, was moved to shed tears for joy."

The picture which our author supplies of Master Robert visiting his unhappy kinswoman, forsaken as she was of her natural comforters, is too fine for curtailment: " A little before his coming she had desired to see her infant before her departure hence to God. I was loath to it at first, fearing lest the sight of him should draw back her heart again after him, and make her wae to leave him; but she assured us that the contrary should be seen, and caused send for him, who was brought her while she was in conference with the said Master Robert. The sight of him altered her nothing from her own course, wherein she continued constant; but she only took him in her arms, and kissing him she blessed him, and recommending him to the Lord's care, who she was assured would be a Father to him, desired Master Bruce to oversee him, that he should be trained up in the fear of God, and sent him away again without taking of any sorrow. After some conference with her, Master Robert departed."

The hour of execution was fixed for early morning, in order to avoid publicity; but a great multitude thronged the Canongate to witness the end, the very house-tops being occupied with people. Confessing her guilt, and beseeching mercy at the hands of the Lord's Majesty for Jesus' sake in a prayer which her spiritual guides had taught her, Jean Livingstone was beheaded by the maiden,[1] on Saturday, 5th July, 1600.

---

[1] An instrument of execution similar to the guillotine, constructed at Edinburgh in 1564-65 and used till 1710.

CHAPTER XI

The Needle that Drew in the Episcopal Thread

AT the Dundee Assembly of 1597 King James, being present in person, persuaded the Church Court to appoint a General Commission " of the most wise and discreet of the brethren, having full authority to consult with His Majesty in all affairs concerning the weal of this Church." Fourteen ministers were elected to this Commission, one or two of them, for the sake of appearances, being of the true blue Presbyterian colour, but the bulk of them men devoted to the policy of the King.[1] It was a false step on the part of the Church, as it was an astute move on the part of James. These Commissioners became a permanent Ecclesiastical Council, having Episcopal powers. " That fatal Trojan horse " was the judgment of Melville's party. And the diarist wrote: " It was the very needle to draw in the Episcopal thread."[2]

Robert Bruce was absent from the Dundee Assembly; his name does not appear upon the records. But he was not deceived as to the purpose of this Commission. And unhappily its very first operation brought him into direct conflict with the new instrument of King James. Two young ministers were selected arbitrarily by the King and his Commissioners to be colleagues of the four ministers of Edinburgh. Great objection was taken to their settlement, partly because of their youth, partly because they were being placed against the wishes of the people. The other members of Presbytery were inclined to content themselves with a simple protest against the method of election. Bruce, however, was made of sterner stuff: he refused to acquiesce in their settlement over the congregations

---

[1] *Booke of the Universall Kirk*, p. 461.
[2] Melville's *Diary*, p. 529.

till he had seen God's blessing upon their labours. A painful
scene occurred at the kirk-session meeting, when Bruce firmly
refused to give the right hand of fellowship to one of the young
men, George Robertson. Upon the latter extending his hand :
" Pardon me," said Master Robert, " I cannot do it till I have
seen some arguments of God's blessing upon your labours; then
ye shall have both heart and hand." Master George, greatly
offended, left the church. The ministers present remonstrated
with Bruce for his carrying matters to such an extreme, whereupon he withdrew, saying he must be the Jonah who was cast
out of the ship. His departure was the signal for Robertson's
return, and the forms of his settlement were carried out with
the aid of the King's new Commissioners. Master Robert Bruce
absented himself from meetings of kirk-session for some time
thereafter. His state of mind is revealed in the following devout meditation, which is given in Calderwood :[1]

" I am lost in very great doubt. Upon the one hand, I am
sorry to leave the children of God in this city : I am sorry to
want my exercise, that presence of God that sanctified me :
and afraid to incur the charge that I left my station, that I
have given over the battle and put up my sword. On the
other side again, I see this manner of entry is not sanctified,
but very corrupt. I see no spiritual authority in them (the
Commissioners) to bear out this work; and if we shall accept
of them at this time, I see a dangerous preparation established
in this city, to be a precedent for all the kirks of Scotland, and
for all the Kings that are to succeed our King, to do the
like.

" If I hold out and accept not, my removing may be a
ground another time to reform the corruption. If I accept, I
cannot see how it can be reformed in any time hereafter. I
like not to abide in their company to whom I am opposed, and
whom I resist in their entry. Rending of actions followeth
rending of hearts. Loath am I to be a spectator and beholder
of such a decay, that have seen the glory of the former work.
What is most expedient I am uncertain. But I am instant

[1] Vol. v. p. 677.

with His Majesty (God) that in the light of His Spirit it may be given me to see which of the two will please Him best, that by His powerful grace I may be resolved to follow the light: yea, I crave also that He who has my heart and tongue in His hand may so govern both that they cast me not in His Majesty's disgrace; but that I may keep His favour and His countenance, with the daily growth of His inward grace, howbeit it were never so far against my affection, bodily ease, and outward commodity. The Lord grant this for Christ's sake."

This beautiful soliloquy reveals clearly the attitude of Bruce towards those whose policy he detested. It reveals more. It is a window through which we can look into his own mind. Here is one who must always set obedience to His Majesty, the King of kings, above any mere courtly submission to his grace, King James. It was Bruce's way both in sermons and in speech to address God as His Majesty. Along with a determination to be loyal to God, there is a sore unwillingness to oppose others. So we behold him standing in great perplexity of mind, the very figure of one who is mystified, yet who by some holy instinct discerns the path of duty.

The very next year a fresh ground of difference arose. The Assembly of 1598 enacted that a rearrangement of the pastorate in Edinburgh must be made, for the better oversight of the growing city.[1] Robert Bruce was present at this Assembly, at which many decisions were come to which grieved him, and against which he lifted up his voice.[2] He welcomed, however, the plan for a more effective supervision of the charge of Edinburgh. When the King asked him, along with his brethren, in presence of the Commissioners, if he was agreed to accept a particular flock, he answered in the affirmative. Great was his surprise to learn in the next breath that his Majesty proposed to insist on his being anew ordained to the ministry, as if his previous nine years were irregular. Some ceremonial, such as the laying on of hands, he would submit to, provided his

---

[1] *Booke of the Universall Kirk*, p. 471.
[2] He opposed the proposal that ministers should have a vote in Parliament.—Cald., v. p. 694.

colleagues were treated in the same fashion; one of them,
Master James Balfour, was in the same position as Bruce.
The latter would have no such process in his instance as might
cast a slight upon his bygone ministry. He could not have
a hand in any procedure which might seem to invalidate all the
administrations of sacraments and ministerial functions of his
pastorate.

The ceremony of ordination to the holy ministry is performed
in the Presbyterian Church by solemn prayer on the part of
the presiding minister, who is called the moderator. At the
moment when he prays " that God Almighty may be with us
as in His name and by the authority of the Presbytery, we
ordain *this thy servant* to the office of the ministry with the
laying on of hands," he, along with those other ministers of
Presbytery who are present, lays his hands upon the head of
the kneeling brother who seeks ordination.[1] Master Robert
Bruce maintained that at an early date, on that day when he
had been called by the unanimous voice of his brethren to dispense the communion, he had received at their hands what
was equivalent to this ordination. If he should submit anew
to the rite, he should proclaim himself to have run unsent,
and to have administered the sacrament without authority
during these eleven years.

There is no doubt that the King and his advisers of the new
Commission believed that, by insisting thus upon a fresh ceremony of ordination, they prepared the way for a later declaration that ordination to the ministry was invalid save at
the hands of a bishop.[2] The process by which Bruce was
tortured and driven between King and Presbyters was extremely painful. No doubt he suffered the consequences of his
former indecision, and refusal to accept of regular ordination.
No doubt a less punctilious man would have acquiesced in the
plan to ordain afresh. His most trusted brethren admitted that
his former ordination had been irregular. They hinted that he
stood too much upon trifles. The King as usual was plausible
when face to face with the minister, but when others had his

[1] 1 Tim. iv. 14.   [2] Scot's *Narrative*, p. 106.

Majesty's ear it was different. Says James Melville with some humour, the two Commissioners appointed to give Bruce the imposition of hands were in dread of the laying on of the hands of the people, who were deeply enraged because of the slight which was proposed towards their minister.[1] Bruce declared himself quite willing to submit to any form of induction to the new pastorate which was consistent with the recognition of his former ministry, and he asked but for a written and signed document to that effect.

This reasonable request appeared to be granted, and on a day we find those Commissioners, to whom the duty was assigned, meeting in the Little Kirk to set Bruce and his colleague James Balfour apart to the ministry of the congregation of the north-west quarter. The King is out at his hunting, and all goes smoothly at first. After the bell has been rung the presiding minister preaches, and conducts what is termed " the Action," or induction ceremony. Thereupon Bruce ascends to the pulpit and harangues the people. The ceremony which he regards as indifferent he will submit to, if only the Moderator and the Commissioners present will sign a statement that this is no new ordaining. The elders, seated on forms around, all join in a loud cry, " We acknowledge him to be our pastor," and then grasp Bruce by the hand. But the Moderator will not consent to Bruce's qualifying words, and the diet ends ineffectually.

The King learnt of all these proceedings next day, and he was angry with Master Robert. The latter was admitted to an audience, and James demanded: " What motion was yon ye made yesterday in the kirk? What mean ye by going up to the pulpit? What said ye in the pulpit? How have ye bewitched the people with your harangues? " I said," calmly replied the other, " that my life was not so dear to me as the honour of my calling." At length the King told him that neither himself nor any of the ministers was of opinion that Bruce had a lawful calling to be a pastor in Edinburgh. The ministers were called and interrogated in succession, and to

[1] *Diary*, p. 419.

the dismay of Bruce it was found that every one of them, even Robert Rollock, held that there was lacking in the case of Bruce what should complete a valid ordination. "Ye have slipped from the cause, and left us out," was Bruce's final word; "as for myself, I thank the living God I am not ashamed of it." He stood up, an Abdiel among the faithless ones.

Technically, no doubt, these men were right, but Bruce felt that he fought the battle of the Church, and he was loath to yield. The Presbytery of Edinburgh, to his great comfort, gave their unanimous judgment that he was a lawful pastor of the Kirk, by whom God in His mercy had wrought effectually; and his life-long friend, Master Patrick Simson, wrote a brotherly letter from which extracts must be given.

"Right honourable and well-beloved brother, I received your letter, wherein I understand that your ministry in Edinburgh these eleven years bygone has been called in question. Dear brother, this is one of Satan's old fetches towards you, who as he was a great hindrance to your entry unto this holy calling, so he leaves not off yet to practise his old and wonted malice against you. But be of good comfort, sir: the Lord, who sees that the drift of Satan is against His own kingdom, will fortify the pillars of His own house that they may stand out against the gates of hell." He regrets that Bruce's own brethren are instruments of the trouble; men who have themselves given good testimony to that ministry. "Ye have a witness in the secret of their hearts that your ministry is of God, and that it hath watered the husbandry of God more fruitfully than the ministry of any man who opposes the same."

Simson concludes by advising his correspondent, if only the Commissioners will approve of his former ministry, not to hold out against the imposition of hands, for as much as it is the command of the General Assembly. "And ye have promised to the King's Majesty (as appears by the writing I received) to do the same; and the hungry souls of the Lord's people earnestly crave the comfort of your ministry. And finally, whatever iniquity be in their hands at this time, I hope the

Lord will pardon it in Jesus Christ, if ye make earnest prayers for them."

What an exquisite tone pervades this letter! What gentleness! What charity! No wonder that this man was a great force for good in the whole Church! But Bruce was of other stuff. He was not easily bent. The threat of deprivation hangs over him. He is found walking one day half a mile beyond the city wall, pondering doubtless upon his dilemma. Another day he retreats to the village of Smeaton, a neighbourhood fragrant with memories of Patrick Hamilton, the martyr, his own mind turning no doubt readily to possibilities of a like fate. Negotiations are protracted, Master Patrick Simson performing the office of intermediary. At one conference Master Robert bursts out in pent-up grief, declaring that he has been persecuted extremely. " And now I take leave of you, my brethren, and wish you from my heart rather to choose affliction than iniquity." At long last admission to his charge was conceded him in the same form as had been used with the other ministers. The King yielded, and on Friday, 19th May 1598, in the Little Kirk, Master Robert Pont, as presiding moderator, after sermon, came down from the pulpit and laid hands upon the heads of Robert Bruce and James Balfour, the elders and deacons seated around upon forms taking them thereafter by the hands and welcoming them as their lawful pastors. Thus a squabble which had been protracted in a most unseemly way for many weeks was at length brought to an end.[1]

But, alas! there were fresh grounds of quarrel arising continually between King and Kirk, and the four old ministers of Edinburgh—Balcanquhal, Balfour, Bruce, and Watson—were special objects of the royal animosity. Novelties in the Church, such as the observing of Christmas, or yet worse the restoring of the Glasgow bishopric, enraged these Fathers, and they spoke their minds according to their wont from the pulpit. The King said that he feared bodily harm, and his fury and his vociferations against them exceeded all bounds.[2] Bruce

[1] Cald., v. pp. 711-723.   [2] Ibid., v. p. 731.

was as usual singled out for exceptional treatment, and the persecution of him, in which his King allowed himself to indulge, became the talk of every stranger in Edinburgh. The English ambassador, in his confidential correspondence with Sir Robert Cecil, declares that the King of Scots was jealous of the remarkable increase of Bruce's popularity in the city and throughout the country, and he avers with regard to the preacher's denunciation of the Glasgow bishop, that his Majesty took this interference of Bruce in worse part than the 17th of December itself.[1]

From the same source we obtain details of a transaction altogether discreditable to James VI, and illustrative of the great lengths of dishonour to which his frenzy impelled him in persecuting Bruce. Ten years previously, on the very week of his sailing to Norway for his bride, he had bestowed on the minister (at that time a great favourite), a life-interest in the abbacy of Arbroath, amounting to twenty-four chalders of wheat. This pension, as it was called, the King now proposed to withdraw. Robert Bruce was no miser, but, like his father, liberal-handed, and when it is told that a portion of this grant was given to a ministerial colleague by Bruce's express request, all reflections upon the latter as over-keen in money matters are satisfactorily disposed of.[2] Master Robert, as first minister of Edinburgh, had a burdensome office to maintain; and besides, when he understood upon what grounds the King proceeded against him, he was hardly the man to take such treatment lying down. The English ambassador, who has been referred to, has scant sympathy with Scottish Church disputes; indeed, he contemptuously styles the ministers "bellows-blowers." Yet it is he who, in a letter written at this time, describes Bruce's self-possession in the pulpit: "He preached this day, as he ever doth, very calmly." In contrast with this calm dignity is set the fury of King James. Master Robert's resolution to resist the act of spoliation above narrated was stiffened when he learnt that it was his Majesty's purpose to

---

[1] *State Papers, Scotland, Elizabeth,* vol. lxii. No. 28.
[2] M'Crie's *Melville,* p. 230, n.

bestow the pension on Hamilton, the same who had dealt falsely with the minister in that matter of "the 17th December." If the revenue he had enjoyed were reserved by the King for his own use, or bestowed upon the Church, he declared himself ready to forego his claim; but otherwise he would contest it in the Courts of law. In due course this pretty dispute found its way into the Court of Session. The report can be read to this day in the Register.[1] In those times this Court met in the Tolbooth. The King had the bad taste to put in an appearance, and he threatened or he coaxed the Lords of Session by turns, taking the very ring from his hand and sending it to one or other of the judges. So hot did his rage burn when he found that the case must go against him, that he shouted concerning his rival: "If I had a whinger I would cast it in his face."

The interlocutor was passed in favour of Bruce, with only one dissentient voice. To the shame of his Majesty be it added, that he hurled from office his Treasurer, Mr. Edward Bruce, because he stood for justice that day. In the end this man suffered banishment to Inverness, and was compelled for the sake of peace to resign his high office.[2] Sir Alexander Seton, the President, was equally resolute. "All honest men," he said, "would vote according to their consciences, or resign."[3] This Seton was a Roman Catholic, and as in later years he formed one of that evil tribunal which sent Welsh and his friends to prison in Blackness, one is glad to be able to record an earlier instance of his courage and integrity. Unquestionably in the years which we describe, justice was tampered with both by influence and by bribes. Master Robert Bruce had been repelled from the profession of law in his youth, because he believed that one could hardly keep oneself untarnished in such a career, and personally he suffered much injustice during his public life. All the more gratifying is it, therefore, to

---

[1] June 16, 1599.
[2] Spottiswood's *Church History*, p. 454; Mr. Andrew Lang, *History of Scotland*, vol. ii. p. 438.
[3] *Memoranda of Sir R. Cecil*, State Paper Office, London, 1599.

record this splendid instance of incorruptibility on the part of the Court of Session in its handling of the appeal of Bruce.

King James the Sixth was not, however, come to the end of his resources: like a fox he had many wiles. "The King swears" (to quote again from the letters of the English ambassador) "he will have Master Robert Bruce's cause reversed; which the Chancellor understanding saith he will pen in Latin, French, and Greek, to be sent to all the judges of the world to be approved, and that by his vote it shall never be reversed." It was a curious quarrel. James took ere long to whining that he could not be sure of his life so long as Bruce remained in the town.[1] Next, he had recourse to petty annoyances. Every Saturday for fifteen weeks, when he knew that the minister was busily engaged in his manse preparing for the Sabbath duty, he sent down messengers for the purpose of interrupting him. At length Master Robert was driven to imploring the Queen's intervention between him and her irate consort, and his friends advised the minister to escape to the continent. It was reported to him that his Majesty had been pleased to declare that he "hated not Bothwell with a greater hatred than he doth you."[2]

By and by a new line was pursued, and the King made a serious attempt to cut off Bruce's regular stipend, and so to starve him out. On a technicality of law the case of the pension came into Court once more, and by a clever ruse it was called while Bruce was absent from town at his mother's funeral. Upon his return, when he learnt what had transpired, he spoke to his King with much dignity of the letter written ten years before by the royal hand, wherein it was declared that he deserved the pension even supposing it had been a quarter of the kingdom. "That writing," said the minister, "I shall keep as a monument to posterity, as your Majesty also bade me."[3] The King was not inaccessible to an appeal such as this, and he replied: "Only save my honour, Master Robert, and I shall not hurt you." The other, quite ready to

---

[1] *State Papers, Scotland, Elizabeth,* vol. lxiv. No. 44.
[2] Cald., v. pp. 734, 735.   [3] *Ibid.,* v. p. 768.

save the wounded *amour propre* of the King, offered once more
to surrender the Arbroath gift absolutely into the hands of his
sovereign upon the conditions previously stated.   But what
King James was pleased to call his honour was a frail reed.
As might have been anticipated, so soon as the minister re-
signed his pension into the royal hands, no more heed was paid
to the conditions which had been laid down by Bruce, who
thereupon threw up the whole business in disdain.

CHAPTER XII

The Matter of Gowrie

" I was twice in France," Bruce wrote in his narrative : " once before my calling; next in my calling, for the matter of Gowrie." By his calling the writer means that spiritual crisis through which he passed in 1581. The visit to France " before his calling " was made as a student about the year 1572. The second visit was paid " in his calling," or during his ministry, when he was banished for the matter of Gowrie in the end of the year 1600.

Bruce was never on the Continent save on those two occasions. Mr. Andrew Lang's statement that he went to Paris in 1599 to bring home the Earl of Gowrie, involving as it does the insinuation that Bruce was accessory to the affair of Gowrie House, is without any foundation.[1]

The Earl of Gowrie was regarded at this time by many Scottish people as the coming leader of the Church party. Trained as he had been under Principal Rollock, he had impressed his friends both on the Continent and at home with his strong Protestantism. It can therefore be well understood that the ministers came to regard the young Earl of Gowrie as the rising hope of their party, and that they were ready enough to suspect foul play in the matter of his death. Robert Bruce, along with the others, had formed the fondest expectations of the career of this Scottish earl, and when these hopes were dashed to the ground all his misgivings shaped themselves in a suspicion, nearly ineradicable, that King James was a sharer in the guilt of Gowrie's death.

But the strange story must be told from the beginning. It

[1] Mr. Andrew Lang's *History of Scotland,* vol. ii. p. 445. (*See* note at end of Chapter.)

will not surprise those who have been able to enter into the secret of Bruce's life to learn that, upon the very night preceding the morning of the tragedy of Gowrie's death, the minister, as he dwelt in his manse at Edinburgh, had one of those premonitions which appear to have been granted to him at the great crises of his career. It seems clear that God in His compassion visited His servant that night, even while he was engaged in his devotions, preparing him by a special grace for the ordeal which impended.[1]

Upon the 5th of August 1600 the King, being resident at the time in Falkland Palace, rode out early in the morning to hunt the stag. The weather was pleasant, the King was a keen sportsman, eager to mount and ride. On this particular morning, however, he was interrupted by a young nobleman, Alexander Ruthven, brother of the Earl of Gowrie, who, approaching him and bowing very low, told His Majesty a strange tale about a great pot of gold coins of which he had gained possession. The object of his tale was evidently to lure the King within the city of Perth, where Gowrie House was situated : and the ruse succeeded. What took place between Ruthven and King James in the little study of Gowrie House, behind locked doors, is one of the unsolved problems of history. On few historic events are there preserved more exact or more picturesque details—the colour of his Majesty's dress, the hunting horn at his belt, the "muirfowl" which was cooked for a hasty dinner, the dish of strawberries, the "skall" that was drunk in a cup of wine. But of the essentials there is only a mass of contradictions. What motives, what aims drew the Ruthven brothers and their King together on that August day? The statement of King James, published over all the land, was that the younger brother attempted to bind him or even to kill him. What is quite certain is that the two Ruthvens, young Alexander and his brother the Earl, were slain, and that James, when the door was burst open, knelt down upon the rushes with which the floor of that little room was littered, and gave pious thanks for his deliverance, adding the

[1] Wodrow's *Life of Bruce*, p. 83.

petition that his life, which had been thus preserved, might be devoted to the welfare of his people.[1]

By the year 1600 the leaders of the Scottish Church had lost all confidence in the word of their King, and James had entered upon that policy of antagonism to the Church which in the next reign upset his dynasty. We need not therefore be surprised that the representatives of the Church harboured grave suspicions concerning the King's complicity in the Gowrie affair. And James VI was clumsy in his effort to convey a particular complexion to the mystery, distinctly overdoing his part, so as only to deepen suspicion. For instance, twenty-four hours after the affair of Gowrie House a royal order came to Edinburgh, commanding the ministers from their pulpits to give thanks not only for his Majesty's deliverance but for his deliverance from treason. Is it to be wondered at that those of the clergy who had the deepest respect for themselves and for their calling declined to obey the order till they had the proofs? Five city ministers, to their credit, point-blank refused. Gladly, of course, did they unite with their brethren, on the Sabbath immediately following the event, in praising God for the safety of the royal person, but till they had evidence of treason they refused to go so far as to assume that. "So the King," says Bruce, "was incensit." So far from complaining of their scruples, we must to-day rather express our amazement that there was any man to be found in the capital, on whom holy hands had been laid in ordination, willing to hire out his conscience in obedience to so unreasonable a command. These five ministers, in the light of history, cut a far more imposing figure than the poor sycophant who held forth at Edinburgh Cross in eloquent words about the innocent lamb (meaning James VI) closed up between two hungry lions thirsting for his blood.[2] If Bruce and his four companions demanded evidence, they were not unreasonable when it was produced. If Bruce was slow to convince, and characteristically unbelieving, his evidence is the more valuable on that

[1] See note, pp. 120-121. [2] Cald., vi. pp. 50-56.

very account. At the bar of history James VI's best witness
is not the sycophant Galloway, it is the sceptical and incor-
ruptible minister Bruce, who in the end, after a slow sifting of
the evidence, expressed himself ready to believe in the innocence of his King.

As for the five[1] who would not comply with the royal order,
the severest penalties were laid upon them. They were forbidden to preach anywhere in Scotland, under pain of death.
They were ordered to leave Edinburgh within forty-eight
hours, and not to show themselves within ten miles of the city.
" They thanked the Lord heartily, and said their sentence was
very welcome, and so departed." " This occasion was gripped
at," says the chronicler of the Church, " to overthrow the
ministry in the capital, which crossed the Court in all its evil
proceedings." " Master Robert Bruce was especially detested
for his uprightness, his fearless correction of evil, his determined opposition to the prevailing policy in the Church."[2]

The wanderings of this last during the weeks that followed
are given in simple, graphic detail in a scrap of that narrative
which has been already more than once referred to. Here we
can follow him as he rides across the country, like one hunted
on the moors: his two body-servants are in attendance upon
him. For a time he stays at "Auld Lady Whittingehame's,"
in East Lothian, then forward to Crailing in Tweeddale, where
he ventured to stay a while, but evidently dreading lest his
presence should compromise those kind protectors, he moved
on, afraid to settle anywhere, aware that he was watched and
that his every action would be reported and misconstrued.
Somehow a fresh summons from the jealous King reaches him
in his wanderings, to appear before the Council at Stirling and
receive a heavier sentence. So we follow this lone rider to
North Berwick and East Fenton; he crosses the water at Earl's
Ferry, "where," says he, " I was very extreme sick." At
Master William Scot's, in Carmurie, despite the need of haste
if he would keep the tryst at Stirling, he rests on the Sabbath

---

[1] They were Balfour, Balcanquhal, Watson, Hewat, and Bruce.
[2] Cald. vi. p. 59.

day. On Monday we find him at Inverkeithing: " I crossed the water at Queensferry; upon the morn, which was Tuesday, I come to the Carse at even." Here he rested for a night, presumably under his own roof at Kinnaird, or in the neighbouring Castle of Airth, where his father had lately died. "And on the morn, which was Wednesday, I role to Stirling, none in company with me, except my two men *and myself*. My brother John convoyed me to the Sauchiefurde, and there left me, and went home."

This is the man who has preferred a conscience void of offence to the favour of kings. And now he has fallen out of favour: men and women are passing him upon the causeway with averted eyes; and he steps onward as lonely as Christian when he entered the Valley of Humiliation. " I rode forward, and there was none in company with me except myself "—and my God. " Alone, yet not alone, because the Father is with me." " Lo, I am with you alway, even to the end."

It is not difficult for us to reproduce that scene in the Castle of Stirling, when the solitary minister enters into the presence of James and his Council, and, holding up his right hand, solemnly swears that he will speak truth.

"First the Chancellor speered where I had been. I said I was in East Lothian. He speered if I was in any other parts. I said I was in the Merse. Then he speirit in what part of East Lothian. I said, Auld Lady Whittingehame's. Then he speirit was I in no other part of the country. I said, yes. I was in Teviotdale. Then he speirit wha was with you in company." Thereupon ensued a close examination of him, the King personally pressing for his acknowledgment (in common with the other ministers) of his Majesty's innocence in the matter of Gowrie. When Bruce came to refer to the corpses of the Ruthven brothers, found lying on the ground, he was so deeply moved that he could not proceed for a time.[1] He was told that his mistrust was due to a preposterous affection for persons. And it is plain that Bruce was much attached to the young Earl of Gowrie; he felt towards him like Beza, who

[1] Cald., vi. p. 84.

wept when he learnt of his untimely fate. Bruce, however, declared before the Council that he had more serious grounds than those of sentiment for his incredulity. The Earl of Mar, always his friend, thereupon took him sharply to task for being so slow to convince. "It is conscience," cried Bruce, "that moves me." And it was in vain that his brethren, or those good noblemen who sought to retain his services in Scotland, or women like the Countess of Mar and the Countess of Morton, attempted the office of peacemakers.[1]

The other four ministers were by this time persuaded of the innocence of King James in the matter of Gowrie's death, and they consented to proclaim this publicly, proceeding from church to church to express their regret that they had doubted, much like penitents purging themselves of guilt.[2] Worthy James Balfour actually submitted to this indignity in the towns of Dundee, Arbroath, Montrose, and Brechin. Bruce could not honestly do it: he had an almost morbid dread lest he should offend his King,—not James VI but Jesus Christ, whose servant he was. And so anxious was he to do no violence to the sanctuary of his own soul that he remained obdurate still. "I am troubled," he wrote to a brother-minister, "for lack of a full persuasion. Now this sort of persuasion is the action of the heart, and God only is the searcher and trier of the heart. The Lord help mine unbelief!"[3] To his wife he wrote: "I would not be in their case for all the benefit they have gotten, for the Court giveth it out that they are sent to make their repentance, each one of them in so many kirks."

There was now no course open to Bruce, firmly refusing as he did to assent to the King's conditions, save banishment from both Scotland and England. King James' influence beyond the border was enough to prevent his finding an asylum there. On the eve of his setting sail he spent a night or two at Restalrig, waiting for the ship that should bear him over to France. So little were disloyal thoughts in his mind that his

---

[1] Cald., vi. p. 95. The Countess of Morton was the wife of that sturdy Reformer, William Douglas of Lochleven.
[2] *Record of Privy Council*, 11th September 1600. [3] Cald., vi. p. 88.

last action, ere he embarked, was to write a dutiful letter to his King: "I am not ignorant of that speech, that the wrath of the prince is the minister of death." And he showed to King James to what length his troublesome conscience would allow him to go in the way of compromise. "Finally," said he, "there is no duty your Majesty can crave of me, without the manifest offence of God and hurt of my own conscience, but I will do it with as good a heart as ever I did anything on earth."

All in vain; the King was, as usual, shifty as a fox, not knowing his own mind; the minister knew his own mind very well, and with many sighs, yet without flinching, he rode down to Queensferry and embarked. It was whispered abroad that the ship, which had been caught in a neap tide, was miraculously floated. An unusual light sufficient to read by at midnight appeared in the sky, as it were guiding the vessel that carried God's faithful servant. So Bruce landed at Dieppe on the 8th of November 1600.[1]

On the shores of France, Bruce vanishes from our view, and we know nothing of the place of his residence, or of his occupations, while he was in exile during the winter 1600-1. The French Reformed Church would gladly welcome an opportunity of showing kindness to a minister of that Scottish Church which had harboured Huguenot refugees in days not long past. And now that the Edict of Nantes, which had been just two years in force, brought a temporary peace to the Protestants of France, the exile from Scotland would find shelter there.

But he does not appear to have thought of settling on the Continent in the manner of so many of his fellow-countrymen. He had not the fluency of his comrade, John Welsh, in speaking the French tongue; when formerly in France or in Flanders he had suffered in his health;[2] and besides, he lacked the power of a man like Master Robert Boyd, of Trochrig, to transfer his heart to a foreign land. The name of John Welsh is to be found to this day upon the minutes of the French Re-

---

[1] Cald., vi. pp. 98, 99.
[2] Wodrow's *Life of Bruce*, p. 94.

formed Church; not so the name of Robert Bruce—he stayed too short a time for that. Had he remained in France a month or two more, so as to attend the synod which met at Gergeau in May 1601, he would have listened then to very familiar discussions anent the propriety of laying on hands at ordination; and he would have been deeply interested in the adopting of an injunction by this same synod as to the handling of the sacred cup: it must be given not by the communicants one to another, passing it from hand to hand, but pastors, and elders assisting the pastors (when they are tired by the multitude of communicants), shall deliver it.[1]

We may be quite certain that Master Robert Bruce, while he continued in France, would exert a gracious influence on behalf of his Lord. It is clear, from a reference in one of Master Patrick Simson's letters, that Bruce exercised his preaching gift while absent from Scotland.[2] In the year 1601 another Scottish ecclesiastic, John Spottiswood, by this time in the enjoyment of his bishopric, crossed over to France; not as an exile he, but in the train of a royal ambassador. Calderwood tells us that he attended Mass, and conformed so far as to kneel down among the worshippers.[3] In the very next page to that in which the historian narrates this instance of bowing in the house of Rimmon, he gives us that letter of Bruce, the unbending Presbyterian, wherein he tells his wife of the circumstances in which he took the sacrament of the Lord's Body in France. It is almost the only fact which has emerged concerning his occupations while in exile. In a characteristic gush of candour he reveals what his emotions and resolves were as he partook of the sacred bread and the wine with his French brethren: "I would rather be banished from England and Scotland by his Grace (the King) than stain the glory of my ministry; let not my union to my Lord Jesus be impaired; let my conscience be without hurt, and the credit of my holy ministry without loss in the hearts of His dear children."[4]

---

[1] Quick's *Synodicon in Gallia Reformata*, vol. i. p. 327.
[2] Cald., vi. p. 137. [3] *Ibid.*, vi. p. 136. [4] *Ibid.*, vi. p. 134.

NOTE ON THE GOWRIE CONSPIRACY

The following account of the incident by a modern writer helps to clarify the author's narrative and has been added by the present publishers.

Ian Finlay, in *Scotland*, Oxford University Press, 1945:

" In 1600, according to James, the son of his old enemy, Ruthven, decoyed him alone into Gowrie House and would have killed him had not his attendants come to his aid and slain Ruthven and his brother first " (p. 40).

Rosaline Masson, in *Scotland the Nation*, Nelson, 1934:

" The Master of Ruthven told James that on the previous evening he had met a suspicious looking man with a pitcher of gold coins under his coat; that he had placed him in ward without telling his brother the Earl of Gowrie, and now he wanted the King to come at once to see him.

" James was fond of gold, but was fonder of a buck hunt, and he demurred. The tale of foreign gold was, however, credible, for Jesuit agents might well carry samples of their bribes; and so it ended in the King's hunting till mid-day, and then, accompanied by the young Master of Ruthven, Ludovic, Duke of Lennox, and others—thirteen in all—riding the twelve miles to Gowrie House, near Perth, to see the man with the treasure. The thirsty King was given wine on his arrival, while dinner was preparing, and after dinner he was taken by the Master up a small stair to a room in a turret, to see the mysterious man. From this point, the only version of the story is what the King told afterwards, for there was no other survivor left to corroborate or deny his tale.

" There was, the King told afterwards, no mysterious man with a pitcher of gold, but a man armed with a dagger, who, when left to guard the King whilst the Master went to fetch his brother the Earl of Gowrie, 'became a slave to his presence,' and, at his request opened a window to allow James to call for help. But the Master returned immediately without the Earl,

and in the struggle that followed, the King managed to shout
'Treason!' from the open window to a group of nobles below.
One of these, Ludovic, Duke of Lennox, looked up and saw
James at the window, red in the face, a hand pressed over his
mouth. They rushed up the main staircase to succour the
King—but were met by locked doors. A ladder, used as a
battering-ram broke. Hammers were fetched, and the doors
battered and broken; but meanwhile, Sir John Ramsay, one of
the King's gentlemen, quicker of thought than the rest, had
dashed alone up the little dark corkscrew stair, broken into the
room, and caught sight of the King and the Master locked together in a death struggle. Sir John drew his dagger and slew
the Master, and he and the King pushed the body down the
corkscrew stair, not knowing whether it were friends or enemies
who were hammering at the other door. From this moment the
story could be told afterwards by others, and was told vari-
ously. A general mêlée ensued—partly within doors, partly
without in the street. During it the Earl of Gowrie was killed,
also by Sir John Ramsay."

CHAPTER XIII

Friends of Bruce at the Court and in the Church

GOD raises up defenders for his own children in the day of their need. Even as it was with Elijah, the prophet for whom friends sprang up at the very Court of Ahab; so was it with Master Robert Bruce. Noblemen and gentlemen, noble women also, espoused his cause, and began to move for his recall from exile. Conspicuous among these, in the difficult months which ensued upon the affair of Gowrie, were John Erskine, Earl of Mar, and his Countess.

Mary Stuart, Countess of Mar, became an attached friend of the holy cause on behalf of which so many brave men suffered and so much Scottish blood was spilt during the first half of the seventeenth century. The conversion of this woman to the cause of the Reformation was unexpected and not without an element of romance. Young Mary Stuart was very beautiful, and extremely like her relative and namesake, the Queen, in personal appearance, if portraits be reliable. Like the unhappy Queen, she was brought up in France in the bosom of the Roman Church. She was a daughter of that adventurer, the Earl of Lennox. Every reader of Scottish history is familiar with the story of John Erskine, the widowed Earl of Mar, almost breaking his heart because this fair girl, only half his age, refused his offer of marriage. Mar, though eight years older than the King, had been educated along with James at Stirling, when George Buchanan was the tutor. The boys became attached to one another, and it is told that James, when he learnt of John Erskine's piteous plight on account of the rejection of his suit, declared, " Ye shall na dee, Jock, for any lass in a' the land "; and he used such arguments with the lady as induced her to change her mind. After her marriage to the Earl of Mar, Mary Stuart was brought under the influence of that godly minister, Patrick Simson, of Stirling, who became the instrument of her conversion to the Reformed faith. She is known as a devoted adherent of the teaching of Samuel Rutherford.[1] A little book of devotions, called *The Sanctuary or Arcadia*, was prepared by a pious minister for the use of the Countess.[2] She befriended John Welsh in his exile in France, and a long letter from his pen makes acknowledgment of her ladyship's sympathy.[3] As for the Earl, Bruce refers in one of his letters with much approbation to the nobleman's religious faith.[4] And his faith was of that sort which stands the severest tests. When Welsh and his comrades were found guilty of treason, he lifted up his voice in protest against the unrighteous judgment.[5]

This pair of sympathisers came forward to interpose on Bruce's behalf, when he retired in 1600 to France. They were in London at the time, where the Earl acted as special ambassador to the Court of Queen Elizabeth, and while there, Lady Mar exerted her influence to obtain leave for Bruce to return. On the arrival of the latter in London in the spring of 1601 he was made welcome to the home of the Mar family. There is a long, interesting, almost gossipy letter from Bruce to his wife, who with the children had spent the winter in Scotland, describing the labours of Lord Mar on his behalf. He tells of his own heart-burning as he sat at dinner in my lord's house. And all unwittingly the writer exhibits in these confidential lines the portrait of a man, hunted, weary, yet obstinate as ever, with his fine distinctions and his points of honour; thirsting for his native-land, yet thirsting even more for the honour of his Master; anxious, if the worst should happen to him, to provide for his children by stripping himself betimes of such possessions as he could transfer. The question in dispute turned upon whether Bruce was fully persuaded of the King's innocence in the matter of Gowrie. " His Majesty," quoth the

---

[1] *Rutherford's Letters*, Ed. A. A. Bonar, Letters 62, 140.
[2] Reprint, Edinburgh, 1862.   [3] Young, *Life of J. Welsh*, p. 326.
[4] Cald., vi. p. 146.   [5] Young, *Life of J. Welsh*, p. 233.

minister to his wife, " chopped aye on that word *fully*; therefore he banished me." " You ask from me such a persuasion
of his Majesty's innocence as I cannot command to the Articles
of my own faith." " What," says my lord, " are you not *fully*
persuaded of the Articles of your Faith?" And we can imagine
the solemnity with which the answer came: " Not, my lord, as
I should be; if you and I both were fully persuaded that there
were a hell, we would do otherwise than we do."

The Earl of Mar was patient with his interesting guest, and
he was painstaking too. My lord answered: " We will not
trouble you with that, neither with conscience, neither with a
full persuasion or resolution. But will you respect the civil
trial, and, seeing that Parliament found certain men guilty in
the matter of Gowrie, will you reverence this judgment?"
" That I shall," replied Bruce, his sense of what was due to the
law overpowering his metaphysical difficulties. An agreement
was patched up, on which the Earl made his report to the
King. The two men travelled north together.[1]

At this point a new difficulty arose, as to whether Bruce
should be requested to proclaim his view of the Gowrie affair
in the pulpit, and the fresh complication resulted in his being
detained for some weeks upon the border, whence he gazed
wistfully upon the promised land of Scotland. Lord Mar, as
a letter of 29th September from the minister of Stirling to
Bruce proves, was unwearied in his efforts at reconciliation.
" Brother," wrote Patrick Simson, " the heart of a King is as
a boat upon the waters, and the Lord stirreth the rudder of it
as His Majesty [God] pleaseth." " Make no delay of your
returning, to the end we may enjoy that benefit of your
presence and ministry, if it please the Lord, which strangers
have enjoyed this time by past."[2] So good Master Patrick
journeyed all the way to Berwick, and, persuading his friend
to conquer his scruples, brought him over the border in triumph. On their arrival in the neighbourhood of Edinburgh,
however, it was found that King James' wretched jealousy
had blazed out anew, and that Bruce was ordered meantime

[1] Cald., vi. pp. 130-135.   [2] *Ibid.*, vi. p. 137.

to restrict himself to the limits of his own place of Kinnaird.

Shortly afterwards a formal order was made that, as Bruce's doubting in the matter of Gowrie had been the principal cause of the doubt of many, the minister should proclaim in the pulpit, at such centres as might be prescribed, the fact that his doubts were now removed. This Bruce stoutly declined to do, and in language worthy of Melville or Knox he replied : " What shall I say? I have a body and some goods; let his Majesty use these as God shall direct him. But as to my inward peace, I would pray his Majesty in all humility to suffer me to keep it, as God of His mercy shall enable me."[1]

Those who assert that the ministers employed their churches in the time of King James VI for the delivery of political harangues will observe here that it is the monarch who demands the putting of Bruce's ministry and Church to such uses, and that the ground upon which the minister refuses is mainly that he has another message than the political to proclaim from the pulpit. Seeking as he did the guidance of God in all his ministry, he found it impossible to turn his vocation to political purposes. " To go through the country and make proclamations here and there, what would this be counted but either due to flattery or to fear."[2]

One of the boasts of King James was, that his chamber door would be made patent to even the meanest minister in Scotland. Accordingly he did not stint Bruce of opportunities to meet him. At Brechin or at Perth or in the Palace of Holyrood, that solitary man stands up single-handed to answer for himself before his King. A letter from the Earl of Mar, commanding him to appear at Brechin to confer with his Majesty, reached him as he was engaged in prayer. The messenger found him on his knees, weeping. It came out in this interview that what had convinced the doubting man of his Majesty's innocence was the oath of Lord Mar. He accepted the nobleman's oath, but he had declined to accept that of the King. It must have been very unpalatable to James to be told thus that his word even on oath was in the view of Bruce unreliable.

---

[1] Cald., vi. p. 141.   [2] *Ibid.*, vi. pp. 141-143.

" I give your version a doubtsome trust," said the minister, quoting from Bernard; " I cannot bring myself to preach it." " All the ministers have done so," said the other, " and ye must not be singular." " Some have not done it," Bruce replied, but when pressed to reveal names he said it would be against the rule of charity to harm my brethren. " Sir, I ought to preach nothing but the Word of God," he kept saying, and everyone who believes with Bruce that God gives His servants a message for the people will understand.

After supper Bruce was given leave to return home. His parting word was one of earnest entreaty to his sovereign that he should not ask honest men to sell their souls. " I understand not what ye mean," retorted the other, " but I shall gar the best of you both say and gainsay." Bruce prayed inwardly all the time thus : " O Lord, keep my heart unto Thee, and save me from the danger that this false and traitorous heart (of mine) is like to cast me into."[1]

In a conference at Perth the two met once more face to face. " No prince," said Master Robert in unmistakable tones, " hath power to give instructions to another prince's ambassador. I am the Son of God's ambassador ! Place me where God has placed me (i.e. in St. Giles pulpit) and I shall teach fruitful doctrine, as God shall give me grace. But we have not had that custom to be enjoined to preach, and I dare not promise to obey that injunction. It lieth not in my hand to make a promise. I know not certainly what God will suffer me to speak. *I have racked certainly a piece of my heart to pleasure your Majesty*. Now, seeing your Majesty cannot be satisfied except I make shipwreck of all, let me go, in God's name." His Majesty at length graciously permitted Bruce to question him upon the details of the Gowrie episode, and the sequel is a unique narrative, obviously reported by Bruce himself, which must be given verbatim.

" Then, first, if it please you, sir," said Master Robert, " had ye a purpose to slay my lord?" " As I shall answer to God," saith the King, " I knew not that my lord was slain till I saw

[1] Cald., vi. pp. 146-148.

him in his last agony; and was very sorry, yea, prayed in my heart, for the same." "What say ye then concerning Mr. Alexander Ruthven?" asked Master Robert. "I grant," said the King, "I am art and part of Mr. Alexander's slaughter, for I did it in my own defence." "Why brought ye not him to justice, seeing ye should have God before your eyes?" "I had neither God nor the devil, man, before my eyes," retorted James, "but my own defence." Here the King began to storm and swear. Master Robert demanded if the King had a purpose that day in the morning to slay Mr. Alexander Ruthven. The other answered, with an oath, that in the morning of that day he loved him as a brother. Master Robert, by reason of his oaths, thought him innocent of any purpose that day in the morning to slay the Ruthven brothers; yet, because he confessed that he had not God nor justice before his eyes, but was in a passion at the time, he could not be innocent before God, and had great cause to repent and crave mercy for Christ's sake.

In the end Master Robert signed a declaration of his faith in King James' innocence, not that he was convinced of this from aught that he knew personally, or from any guidance granted him by God through prayer. But the Courts of his country had adjudicated, and as a subject he would respect these till God gave him further light. The exact words to which he put his name were these: "I am resolved of his Majesty's innocency, and of the guiltiness of the Earl of Gowrie and his brother, according as it is declared by Act of Parliament; and therefore acknowledge the great mercy of God towards his Majesty and to the whole Kirk and country in his Majesty's deliverance." Official permission was accordingly granted him to travel where he pleased, save that he must not approach within a radius of four miles of the capital.[1]

It must not be thought that throughout these conferrings Bruce's best advisers approved of his uncompromising attitude

---

[1] Cald., vi. pp. 153-156. Calderwood omits the statement given above, to which in the end Bruce signed his name. It will be found in *The Booke of the Universall Kirk*, p. 526.

towards the King. Not only the Earl of Mar, but his trustiest friends amongst the clergy, such as James Melville, advised Bruce to consult the path of reconciliation. An Assembly, the last at which King James was to be present in Scotland, met in Holyrood in November 1602, at which the matter of Bruce's treatment arose through a petition on the part of his sympathisers in Edinburgh to secure his restoration to them. Soon it came out that the King was determined on two things,—to exclude Bruce from his old pulpit of St. Giles, and to prevent him and others like him from having a voice in the Assembly. The minister on this occasion left his house in Stirlingshire, and approached Edinburgh. His friends, headed by George Heriot, the goldsmith, were busy on his behalf. But the Assembly, without calling him or giving him a hearing, decided as the King wished, that the first step must be his declaration from his pulpit of his belief in the royal innocence. At the close of the Assembly his brethren held a conference with him by the King's command, and the meeting took place outside the city in the Sciennes. They told him plainly that they considered he stood upon trifles. James Melville courteously urged that the Assembly's injunction should have the effect of making it easier for Bruce to utter what his Majesty desired. Master Robert appeared to acquiesce, and craved leave in the whole matter to seek the guidance of God. In this happy mood he was escorted within the city gates, which he had not crossed since the day of his gallop eastwards into the Merse a twelvemonth previous.

An interview with the King, however, convinced him that though he should concede what his brethren along with his Majesty asked, there would be no leave given him to resume his former ministry. It was ominous that the town officials declined to take for his use the rooms which he had formerly occupied. He was compelled, like his Master at Jerusalem, to retire outside the city wall over night for a shelter. We can follow his steps as he retires one night to Restalrig, another night to Smeaton. Who may have been his entertainers in these villages we are not told, but one kind host, Sir John

Cranstoun of that Ilk, harboured the wanderer for eight days.
" He hath been a succourer of many, and of mine own self
also."[1]

There is one figure at the Court which stands out conspicuous at this time of suspense—that of Sir James Sempill, of
Beltrees. He was a cousin of Bruce; his services were ever at
the disposal of the Church, and at this date he attempted the
difficult rôle of intermediary between his kinsman and the King.

Sempill's position at the Court of Holyrood was unique. His
mother, a daughter, like Bruce's own mother, of the Lord
Livingstone, was no other than that Mary Livingstone who, as
one of the " four Marys," was maid of honour to Mary, Queen
of Scots. Her son, this James Sempill, was of almost the same
age as James VI and had the honour of receiving the royal
name, as well as that of sharing in the studies of the boy-King,
under George Buchanan. Sir James Sempill turned out not
only a good Latin scholar, but a zealous supporter of the
Church, and his " Defence of Andrew Melville " was a real
service to the good cause. He used his influence at Court to
relieve Melville's sufferings, and it was he who obtained for
that most learned Scotsman of his time the use of writing
materials in his prison within London Tower, as well as
permission to see his friends. Melville's gratitude for these
attentions knew no bounds. Speaking of Sempill, he says:
" The Court does not contain a more religious man, one who
unites in a greater degree modesty with genius, and a sound
judgment with elegant accomplishments. I am persuaded that
he takes a warm interest in the cause."[2]

Sir James, as he was mindful of the claims of conscience,
was not forgetful of the ties of blood. His duties of reconciler
were by no means easy. He obtained from the King a definite
promise that Bruce should be restored to his own church, provided he would proclaim his Majesty's innocence on first entering the pulpit. Beltrees, as will be seen from the following

---

[1] Cald., vi. pp. 160-190; *Booke of the Universall Kirk*, pp. 525,
526.
[2] *Melvini Epistolæ*, p. 78.

E

extract, was not a blind partisan of the minister: "So, sir,"
he writes to Bruce, " I think his Majesty dealeth with you most
graciously, and I pray you, sir, for God's cause take away all
offence on either side in the matter of the King. And because
I see I must retire home for a short while myself,[1] ye shall do
well in my judgment to retire home also, upon the excuse I
have made to his Majesty already, till I return: at which time
I will begin anew to entreat his Majesty in your favours, as I
have ever found him favourable. In the meantime I would
wish you to exercise yourself in preaching, and so to behave
yourself towards your neighbours, that thereby they may make
good reports to be carried to his Majesty's ears touching you,
which will make a smooth way to you for your entry into
Edinburgh."

Bruce, as we have seen, had reason to form a less sanguine
view. "If it be the will of the Lord," prayed he, " to pull the
people and the ministry both from me, may it please the Lord
to triple His Spirit upon me, and let me see in my heart His
face brighter and brighter." From his own house in Stirlingshire, to which he had now retired, he wrote to his cousin. The
sufferer, tortured so long on the rack, cries out in his agony :
" These four or five years bygone I have been continually
under a lingering and declining death, which I am assured
hath been more troublesome and tedious to me both in body
and mind than that hour of death shall be whenever it shall
please the Lord to call me thereto; . . . I would promise by
God's grace, whenever the word should give occasion, to sup-
press all sinister constructions of his Majesty's actions."

The next incident is the riding out of a deputation to Stirlingshire to demand why Master Robert did not return to his
pulpit. " It is not obedience to the Act of Assembly that you
seek," cried he, " but only my disgrace, which is the ready
way to make my ministry unprofitable." Soon it became evident to all that Bruce's view was the true one, and that the
King's advisers really were on the watch for an opportunity to
sever the tie that bound the minister to his flock in St. Giles.

[1] To Renfrewshire, where his residence was, in the town of Paisley.

George Heriot and another ventured into the royal presence to intimate that on their suggestion Bruce had returned to the city, and was lodging in the West Port. Upon this James broke out into language of fearful profanity, and the decent citizens regretted that they had brought the minister up from the country. They hurried him beyond the gates, and in a dignified letter which he despatched to the city of Edinburgh, of date, Glasgow, 10th March 1603, he takes a final farewell, shaking off the dust from his feet for a testimony. "I chose rather to retire with the peace I had already gotten than to do anything whereof I was not well resolved as yet how it might stand with the good pleasure of my God. If I should promise any other thing I might well procure the wrath of God, and kindle a fire within my own conscience. I desire as a free man of God to go free!"

The conclusion was as James' "led horse,"[1] the Commissioners, desired. The most fruitful Edinburgh ministry of that generation was brought to an end.

In the year 1603 King James succeeded to the throne of England. On that occasion Bruce ventured to "come east" and offer his congratulations to his Majesty. The King, hearing that he was in town, was ungenerous enough in that hour of his triumph to insist that if there was to be any reconciliation, the minister must ask his pardon upon his knees. Bruce was bitterly disappointed, and was preparing to return to his country retreat, when some good angel whispered worthier thoughts to the King, and he despatched a messenger early in the morning to summon Bruce into his presence. The messenger found Master Robert in bed, and the worthy man was quite vexed for the honour of his cloth that he was not up when the summons came. As he waited in an ante-chamber for audience he prayed (as was his wont) for divine guidance. He would not kneel to the King, but he had carefully prepared a speech to be addressed to his sovereign. James Melville, to whom he had rehearsed his address, heartily approved of it.

We can restore the whole ensuing scene from Calderwood's

---

[1] A title constantly given by the historian of the Church to them.

inimitable pages. It is the early morning hour; the King is at
breakfast. A group of whispering courtiers is seen in the background, among them certain recognisable men—Sir Patrick
Murray, the Earl of Mar, the Laird of Dunipace. After breakfast there is " preaching, which was very cold." Now, the
King, booted and spurred, prepares to ride. He stamps about
" in a circle as his custom is." And now is Master Robert's
opportunity. Very humbly, but declining with characteristic
doggedness to bend the knee, he approaches and delivers his
speech. The God of heaven and earth, he said, had placed his
Majesty on these earthly thrones. Making happy reference to
the circumstances which had led up to this glad consumma-
tion, he bade the King take heed to his own heart, and directed him upward to the crown which cannot fade. Finally,
he bade him in gratitude to God give his whole care to the
preservation of His one kingdom.

James answered: " Master Robert, by God's grace I shall
not place my comfort in any earthly thing"; and his assurances upon public policy were equally satisfactory to his subject. Bruce considered that he had that day as good countenance of the King as ever he had in his life. There was no
word about his kneeling down to confess any fault. God put it
clean out of his Majesty's heart.

Upon James' mounting on horseback, Master Robert approached him again to take leave, and was as well received as
any subject of his profession in the kingdom. One wishes that
the closing remark which bystanders attributed to his Majesty
were according to fact: " Now all misunderstanding is at an
end between you and me, Master Robert."[1]

[1] Cald., vi. pp. 216-219.

CHAPTER XIV

Concerning the Character of Robert Bruce

THE present is a good point of vantage whence to survey the character of Robert Bruce, of Kinnaird, as a whole. It is no part of the duty of a biographer to idealise the person whom he describes. The flaws of Bruce's character have not been concealed in the pages of this book; they are very obvious to every student, but they are quite cast into the shade by his virtues, so that the present chapter is in the main an appreciation.

The personal appearance of Bruce was striking. It is not difficult to form a mental picture of that tall princely form. He came of a race splendid in outward appearance, as they were singularly gifted in the inward parts. His external resemblance to King Charles I will be readily marked by those who compare the portraits of the two men. The common ancestor of these two, King Robert the Bruce, was royal even in his personal presence, and there is another scion of the family, James Bruce, of Kinnaird, the Abyssinian traveller, in whom one can trace many resemblances to Robert Bruce the Reformer. James Bruce, who was a descendant in the direct line of the Kinnaird branch of that family, dwelt at Kinnaird House one hundred years after the minister, and his grave, marked by a tall monument, is not far distant from that of the other, in Larbert Kirkyard. These two Bruces were similarly endowed with a spendid physique. Witty Fanny Burney, a contemporary of the traveller, declared that he was the biggest man she ever saw gratis. Reversing the order of the other, this Bruce gave up the Church for the law; but neither did the Scottish Bar retain his services. Delicate health, together with an inward restlessness, constrained him to travel abroad. The two

Bruces had a like strength of character. There is a strain of melancholy traceable in both, and a subjective tendency which took the form in the one man of morbid self-analysis, in the other of personal vanity. One even inclines to attribute to the minister a taste for nature, such as was characteristic of the famous traveller. Not only did Master Robert Bruce, like St. Francis, see visions of birds, "many black fowls," but one recalls a delightful story of a pyot's nest, which he turned aside to examine because he thought it curiously made. The movement saved him from the bullet of an assassin.[1]

Than Master Robert Bruce, of Kinnaird, there is nowhere a more transparent or more recognisable character within the whole splendid gallery of Scottish confessors. It should not be beyond our power, therefore, to describe him, with his outbursts of candour and his exquisite gift of self-revelation. Through the piety of his admirers we have before us a volume of his sermons, and we have more than a dozen of his letters, full of personal allusion. Portions of the Narrative written by him in his old age have been recovered. His friends have talked frankly about him; and finally, there is preserved a series of interviews which took place between James VI and Robert Bruce, whereby there is revealed to us amazingly the peculiar turn of the minister's mind. On the whole, this portrait of Bruce discloses a man of commanding intellectual gifts, of iron resolution; stubborn, and even what the Scots call "thrawn," a man of great practical gifts, unwearied in the service of the Church, and in the effort to advance Christ's kingdom; emotional, affectionate, devoted to every cause which he espoused, implacable towards the enemy; chiefest of all, a great Christian, in daily fellowship with the spiritual world; earnest in Bible-study and the practice of prayer; one who, as he himself expressed it, "lived by the faith of the Son of God."

When we add to all these great moral and intellectual gifts Bruce's command of influence on account of his family name, it becomes clear that such an one as he was bound to leave a trail upon the page of history. He occupies a place midway

[1] See further, Chap, xv. p. 147.

between Andrew Melville his master and Alexander Henderson his greatest disciple. The history of Scotland in the sixteenth and seventeenth centuries was the history of the Church, and the career of a great Churchman like Bruce cannot be ignored by those who would appreciate the formative influences of that period. Other men there were in the Church of a more plastic type than he. Robert Rollock, Principal of Edinburgh University, was a man of God and a preacher of great power, but he was no statesman, and his easy acquiescence in the policy of the Court was disapproved by the leaders of the Church. There were men, too, of the type of Patrick Galloway, King's preacher and sycophant; men defective in personal conviction, who must be classed with them that betray the pass in the day of battle. Master Robert Bruce is the man who more than any, save Melville, stood up like a tower, unshakable to the very end. He was not vehement, like David Black of St. Andrews, or like John Davidson, whom a certain statesman described as " un petit diable." Bruce had that dogged tenacity which in the end beats down all opposition, the strength of the anvil which breaks many hammers. That gracious spirit, Master Patrick Simson, of Stirling, would have called Bruce stubborn. Bruce says of himself that he was marked with the mark of obstinacy. It is the most obvious quality of his nature; for the most part, when it is harnessed to the yoke of Christ for the doing of His will, this is Bruce's strength; sometimes, however, it becomes a fault, a weakness, dragging the minister into an attitude of dour, unreasoning opposition. Let us not forget, however, what Bruce's stubbornness cost him. He did not take, like some, the path which led to the royal favour and a bishopric. By playing the courtier's part Bruce could certainly have become a great statesman or ecclesiastic. But early in his life he had heard that voice which when once a man has heard he cannot cease to hear it, the voice within his own breast summoning him to obedience. He was a subject quite frankly and transparently loyal to King James; yet for him there was " another King, one Jesus," who must always take precedence of James the Sixth.

It may be said that Bruce failed as a courtier. At least he was not given to flattering kings, and in this connection it must be kept in mind that Scottish kings were not usually addressed in the style in which courtiers addressed Elizabeth. Bruce was always dignified and courtly in his approach to James, while he did not allow himself to forget that he was a servant of Christ as well as a subject of the King. " The strength of the ministers," says Gardiner, whose review of this period is very just, " lay in the undeviating firmness with which they bore witness for the law of God as the basis of all human action, and the vigorous and self-denying activity with which they called upon all who would listen to them to shake off the bonds of impurity and vice." And Mr. Andrew Lang himself handsomely declares that the rudeness (as he calls it) of the ministers is not so repulsive as the flattery of the peers and divines of England.[1] The King's party are, in comparison with the Churchmen, quite without character, such souls as Dante condemns to hard penalties in the Inferno.

Conspicuous among the qualities of Bruce's mind should be set the deep vein of scepticism which pervaded his teaching, while it affected also his practical life. In this respect he stands out among his generation, for there are few signs of the prevalence of intellectual doubt among the men of his time, though the malady is common in our day. Scapegraces were more numerous than sceptics among the subjects of the 6th James; credulity rather than doubt was the enemy. The good-man's croft was still kept, untilled and unsown.[2] Belief in witchcraft, and the torture of those accused of being witches, were common. Bruce dwells in a totally different world from that of the prevalent superstitions. He was a man assailed in his early years with doubt as to the very being of God,[3] one who ap-

---

[1] *History of Scotland*, vol. ii. p. 472.

[2] It was a pre-Reformation superstition to leave a portion of ground untilled by the plough and dedicated to the devil. This was called the " Goodman's croft," the devil being so named to avoid provoking him; by thus placating him a good return would be secured from the rest of the field! See Cald., v. p. 326.

[3] See Blair's *Autobiography*, p. 40.

proached every problem of life from the splendid position of intellectual quest and mastery. He was not one who could accept either his religious or his political creed from the hands of others. Only through the wilderness of doubt could he enter into the promised land.

This strain of scepticism was both his weakness and his strength. It told on his preaching, giving him a message acceptable to such as walked through the dark valley of unbelief. Great passages such as that on " How to pacify the conscience," or his doctrine, " A wounded conscience must ever doubt," are the ripe fruit of the preacher's own experience.[1] The note of emphasis and solemn conviction which hearers marked in his message is derived from his having fought his way to every truth upon which he planted his soul. Some people can believe far too easily. They are more certain of everything than others can be of anything. Doubting may be the condition of the soul's entrance into the possession of a larger, stronger faith.

This inherent scepticism of Bruce had very practical consequences. It did not hinder him from possessing a resonant gospel message, for early in his life he cut his way out of all the meshes both of superstition and of unbelief, to the Cross of Christ. But traces of this infirmity of scepticism are found upon Bruce's everyday life, explaining that curious hesitancy exhibited by him upon critical occasions, when he found himself driven forward beyond the range of his own experience. It is St. Thomas of the Scriptures redivivus. " I am troubled," he writes in a crisis of doubt,—" I am troubled for lack of a full persuasion. The Lord help mine unbelief."[2] Or recall that extraordinary interview in London with the Earl of Mar, wherein Bruce harps like some casuist upon the term " *fully* persuaded." "Not, my Lord, as I should be; if ye and I were both *fully* persuaded that there were a hell, we would do otherwise than we do."[3]

[1] See *Robert Bruce's Sermons*, by John Laidlaw, D.D., p. 195, etc.
[2] Letter of Bruce, Cald., vi. p. 88.
[3] Bruce's Letter to his Wife, Cald., vi. p. 131.

Bruce's extreme and almost morbid culture of his conscience has to be taken into account if we would understand his character. The history of his conversion is an explanation of the stern and overawing sense of sin which mastered him. It would be scarce an exaggeration to quote the instance of Dante, and to say that " this is a man who has been in hell." He has a deep sense of guilt and of sin, and the experience through which he passed gave him an exceptional power in dealing with cases of conscience. While there is a danger from the constant prying into one's own subjective conditions, keeping the finger upon the pulse of the soul, yet they who have had so deep a sense of sin that they have been driven from very fear to the Cross of Christ, prove themselves skilled healers of the wounds of others,—acquainted with the disease and also with the one remedy. What a terrible neighbour is a live conscience! And how good a physician is He who has an effectual cure for fear and doubt and despair. Such an one is Christ, and Bruce had found Him a Saviour able to salve his own wound; therefore he became mighty to interpret the word that saves, and ready also to diagnose the cases of those who sought his help. The most ineffectual of beings is the man who, being aware of sin, does nothing for its alleviation or its cure. The most splendid ally and the most formidable antagonist is the man who both perceives the malady and is aware of a cure. The practical mystic is a tremendous force in the Church. Such is Robert Bruce : one who can move the hearts of men by his gospel message; one who, if he is permitted to be nought else, is a drag upon the wheel, serving to arrest them that hurry the Church into perilous paths.

It must be borne in mind that, with every other quality of mind and heart, Bruce was first and foremost a theologian of great distinction. So competent a judge as M'Crie states that he was a man of stronger mind than Rollock; and these two, Bruce and Rollock, are classed by the same authority as the foremost theologians of their age.[1] It is to be kept in mind that the best intellect of Scotland was found within the Church,[2] so

[1] M'Crie's *Life of Melville*, p. 387.   [2] Gardiner, *Hist.*, i. p. 46.

that there can have been few men better equipped than Bruce to serve his country in the age in which he lived. The gifts and the graces which he commanded were placed at the disposal of the Church whole-heartedly. He was a pronounced Calvinist in his theology, a preacher of the first rank, an ungrudging labourer to win his fellow-countrymen to Christ. We cannot read carefully the sermons or the fragments of Bruce's Narrative which remain, without feeling that we are brought into contact with a mind of the first order, one also which has been yielded in captivity to the service of the Blessed Master. One of the ablest of modern theologians has pronounced Bruce's sermons on the sacraments " classical, monumental, and complete."[1]

But surely the quality which is most conspicuous of all in the life of Master Robert Bruce is that of saintliness. It has been asserted that the Scottish Church has produced few saints. Those whom Scotland canonises in the only valid way, by enshrining them in her heart, are certainly not after the pattern shown us in the orthodox " Lives of Saints." In the story-books your saint has very little colour or character. Robert Bruce was no saint in that negative sense. He was a man of intensely full and varied nature, who brought his passions and his ambitions into subjection to Christ. If by a saint is meant a man of great elevation of mind, one who knew and loved Christ, one who was willing to suffer the loss of all things for Christ, and who shaped his life according to the pattern shown in the Mount of Beatitudes, then Robert Bruce is among the saintliest of men. And it should be quite unnecessary for us to turn to Rome or to Constantinople in quest of holy men, so long as a figure so strong, so saintly, as this presents itself to us in the pages of our own national history.

[1] Dr. John Laidlaw.

CHAPTER XV

The First Exile to Inverness

THE popularity of Bruce in Edinburgh made it advisable to remove him to a distance from the capital, and the first proposal was that he should be placed as a chaplain in some great house in the north. A curious practice obtained in the kingdom at this time of placing representatives of the Church in the houses of great Catholic families with a view to their instruction, and, if it might be, to their conversion. The houses of Huntly and Errol are specially singled out in one Act of Assembly,[1] and the Queen's own palace is actually designated as a point where attentions of this kind might be needed. It was the proposal of King James himself that Robert Bruce should be dispatched north, " to travel with " the Catholic leader, Huntly, for this purpose. The post was a very dangerous one, somewhat like a West African governorship in the last century. If one accepted, he did so with a feeling that he would probably never return. Strathbogie, the Huntly centre, was infested with enemies of the Reformers. What security for Bruce's safety could there be in the dominions of Huntly? It was only the failure of the Earl to meet the minister at James' Court in Falkland that nipped this ingenious scheme in the bud. The royal will was undisguised. James desired to remove Bruce to a distance in the north, to rid himself once for all of the censures of a troublesome subject.

On 27th February 1605 the Church Commission, the King's " led horse," ready as always to register the wishes of the sovereign, removed Bruce from his Edinburgh charge, and forbade his preaching anywhere. Master John Welsh, the

[1] *Booke of the Universall Kirk*, pp. 509, 510.

minister of Ayr, denounced this high-handed action, declaring that the removal of those lights, such as Bruce, who were wont to shine in the land, was a more fearful token of God's wrath than the pestilence which had been in the country for two years. The proud, sensitive spirit of Bruce, under the sting of this treatment, greatly needed sympathy, and it is probable that Welsh added to his kindness by paying his brother minister a visit at Kinnaird.[1] Other and yet more comforting visitations were granted to the sufferer. Riding into Stirling one day, his thoughts troubled him greatly, and, as was his wont, he laid the case before his God ere he went to rest. In the night he had a dream by which it was communicated to him that in the way of obedience to the will of his God he should find safety and peace of soul. This direction of his path through the medium of dreams and premonitions is quite characteristic of the man. And we shall find that clearer indications of the Divine approval were granted him, as he gave new proofs of obedience to his God, and of surrender to the tremendous ordeal of suffering. Surely such was to be expected; for God has promised to give Himself in rich measure to those who yield themselves to Him.

Bruce seems to have paid no attention to the prohibition of the Church Commission; he continued during the summer of 1605 to preach as he found opportunity. If the Church of St. Giles was shut against him, other openings were made, and it was about this time that the kirk-session of Glasgow, as their records still attest, earnestly craved that Master Robert Bruce would teach the word of God for a time in the High Church of Glasgow.[2] We are not informed whether he responded to this invitation from the west. His influence in the west country was very great. He had a large following in Ayrshire. His own residence of Monkland became the centre of a great religious rally.

The success of James in depriving the minister of his pulpit

---

[1] Young, *Welsh's Life*, p. 144.
[2] Now known as the Cathedral. *Glasgow Kirk-Session Records,* February 9, 1604.

in the capital only issued in the defeat of the King's object;
for it resulted in Bruce having recourse to those irregular meetings called "fasts" and conventicles, sometimes conducted in
private houses, at other times in the open air, which heralded
the Covenanting movement. Those who sought the ministry
of men like Livingstone, Dickson, or Bruce found that they
could enjoy it only in this irregular way, and they cannot be
blamed if they forsook the churches, where lifeless doctrine
was taught, for the company of these undoubted apostles of
Christ.

It was not without a conflict that a man trained as Bruce
had been, having so high a conception of what was due to
authority, made his way to the point of sanctioning those
irregular meetings. In a conference with the Chancellor he
yielded to the entreaty of Seton that he should refrain from
preaching for nine or ten days, deeming that concession a
small matter. Whereupon all his tender scruples began to
assail him, and he had a vision which terrified him. "How
durst ye make a promise?" demanded a voice in the night.
"Why did ye not advise with My mouth, and seek My warrant?" The anxiety threw him into a fever, and it was only
when he had avowed an implicit obedience to his God that he
obtained relief. Because of his promise he felt himself debarred from entering the churches, such as the kirk at Larbert.
This appears to be the explanation of Calderwood's statement
that the sequel was Bruce's turning to preach in the open air.[1]
First at the wood-side, on his own estate of Kinnaird, and
thereafter at a neighbour's house where sickness had broken
out, he conducted service. The neighbour was Lord Elphinstone, who had caught the pestilence, and Master Robert
preached before him and Lady Elphinstone, as it were in
quarantine in their garden. If there was not room for God's
servant within the churches, he could find an opportunity, as
his Master had found, under the open sky.

Upon 18th August 1605 the blow fell which Bruce had for
months anticipated, and he was ordered within ten days to

[1] Cald., vi. p. 279.

ward in Inverness. Little time was left him for preparation, for the journey would occupy some days. But the authorities were determined, and the reasons which they offered are significant. In addition to the old sore of the Gowrie affair, there were allegations that Bruce had numbers of ministers and people gathering around him, that he made a habit of criticising the King and the Parliament, as well as the ministry of the Church in his meetings, that he fostered divisions. In short, the popularity of Bruce and the sympathy provoked on his behalf through his persecutions enraged the King. He therefore was resolute once for all to rid himself of this censor who refused to be suppressed.

During a portion of this year Bruce was cast into prison in a deep vault of the rocky islet of Inchgarvie.[1] That little isle on the Forth forms to-day a resting-place for the modern Forth Bridge, and is known to every traveller. It was at this very time that John Welsh and his five colleagues were imprisoned, each in solitary confinement, within that " foul hole " the Castle of Blackness. One of their sympathisers, a lady, consoled them with the happy reminder that " the darkness of Blackness was not the blackness of darkness."[2] While Welsh and his friends lay for fourteen months in their prison, some influence was used to obtain release for Bruce out of Inchgarvie, after a more brief incarceration. We find him by the end of August entering the city of Inverness, where he remained " in ward " for eight years, returning after a brief interval of liberty for a second banishment.

The state of the Highlands in the opening of the seventeenth century was lamentable, and one of the chief problems which confronted the government was the pacification of clansmen, and the quelling of feuds which had become scandalous. Mary Queen of Scots, with her half-brother the Good Regent, had visited Inverness in 1562, " after a journey terrible both for man and beast "; King James VI visited it in 1589, with some purpose of reducing the clansmen to order.

[1] Forbes' *Records*, p. 409.   [2] *Select. Biog.*, vol. i. p. 342.

But he spent most of his time in the north at the chase. Meantime bloodshed, rapine, the burning of farmsteads and hayricks, every sort of lawlessness prevailed. Huntly against Sutherland, and Sutherland against Caithness, the clansmen strove, levying troops and declaring war in savage independence of the government.

King James' policy was one of matching the chiefs one against another; in the case of the fierce clan Macgregor, the edict was that they should be exterminated like vermin. By an act of the year 1603 the very name of Macgregor was wiped out, and in order to escape from pursuit the unhappy bearers of this name were forced to change it, at least for the time. In the same year, 1603, a band of Macdonalds of Glengarry, on a raid into Ross-shire, surprised a party of their enemies in church. Neither religion nor humanity could restrain them. They set fire to the sacred building, burning to death men, women, and children without pity. An additional touch of horror is conveyed by the statement that Glengarry's piper drowned the shrieks of those within the church by playing the marching song of his clan.

The Church, indeed, was becoming alive to some extent to the urgency of the Highland problem. In 1597 a deputation was sent north to inquire into the religious state of the Highlands. One of the deputies was James Melville, and in his pages is found a description of the nature of their operations, the reluctance with which he went north, the need either of admonishing or encouraging the men who laboured in the Highland parishes; the dealing also of his deputies with noblemen and with barons, whose duty it was to provide churches upon their estates. The clan leaders were responsive, and the Mackintosh, or Mackintoshie as he is usually called, excelled all the rest in/ zeal. He met the Church deputation at Inverness, and submitted a plan for his country. " Send us men," said he, " and we shall give security for their personal safety, as well as promise obedience to their doctrine and discipline. Their stipends, too, shall be paid.[1] The Tutor of Sutherland,

[1] Melville's *Diary*, p. 434.

Sir Robert Gordon, was also an encourager of the cause, a good man and a repairer of churches.[1] It would not be expensive to provide or to restore churches, three hundred years ago, for the ecclesiastical architecture was of the simplest, parish churches being frequently roofed with thatch.[2]

James Melville concludes with the statement that the visit to the north was of some service, and that he gained an impression while in those regions that if Christ were preached among them there would be a response such as might put to shame the Church of the Lowlands. Bruce, however, had not been in contact with the clansmen, and knew of them only by hearsay. Consequently his feelings with regard to the condition of civilisation beyond the Grampians were not sanguine. In more than one of the published sermons he has used the Highlands as an illustration. Speaking of the enemies of the Kirk, his words are these: " God makes each one of them to be hangman to the others, as ye see commonly in our Highlands." To a home-loving Scot of the period the sentence of detention at Inverness was like Siberian exile to a Russian of the present time. Master Robert Bruce, who loved his wife, his children, his acres, his beautiful home at Kinnaird House, shrank from the ordeal of his banishment. He could have said, like Bunyan when he passed through a similar trial, " It was like tearing the flesh from my bones." He did not know that the wrath of man should praise God, and that he was ordained to be a pioneer apostle of the north. Nor did the King know, when he sent the great preacher to Inverness, that he was embarking on a policy which should bring peace to the mountains and the glens, not through extermination, but through the instilling of a new principle of love.

Before the removal of Bruce to the capital of the Highlands in 1605, the great fertile territory of Moray, Inverness, and Ross was still largely untouched by the Reformation, and

[1] *History of the Earldom of Sutherland,* pp. 399, 400.
[2] See Row, *History,* p. 12; *Coronis,* p. 471. The roof of Carnock Church was " theiket with heather."

was penetrated by a sort of Popery which was simply baptized paganism. The vicar of Bower in Caithness, about 1613, was a Richard Merchison. It is related with regard to this faithful man, that he went to Wick and, in protest against the image-worship of saints which prevailed there, broke in pieces the image of St. Fergus, patron-saint of the town; whereupon the furious inhabitants seized him and drowned him in the river.[1] Few of the ministers in these counties were possessed of the spirit of the Reformers. King James found from among them the most staunch supporters of his design to overthrow the Church's liberties. At the Perth Assembly of 1596 James Melville tells how a horde of Highland and Aberdeenshire men descended upon the Church Court; " so that my eyes saw a new sight, and my ears heard new voices."[2] By the support of these, King James was able to outvote the men of Fife and the Lothians, amongst whom the strength of Melville's party lay. A Bishop of Moray, writing to King James in 1618, declares that his diocese is so far free of any who will not conform to the articles of Perth, agreed to in that year.[3] In the year 1605 things were not so unfavourable to the church in the diocese of Moray as they became later on. It is significant that among nineteen ministers who met at Aberdeen, in defiance of the royal proclamation, one hailed from Nigg near Tain. The leaven of evangelical truth was penetrating even into the Far North.

The city of Inverness, at the date of Bruce's first arrival in it, was but a small town, made up of two intersecting streets, huddled under the shadow of the castle, which dominated all the neighbourhood. A bridge of oak spanned the river Ness, on the left bank of which was springing up a modest little suburb; there were few of the comforts of life to be found in this remote region. No doctor was within reach, a serious consideration to Bruce, as his health had given way under the strain of his hardships.[4] Lodgings were difficult to obtain. For

---

[1] Auld, *Ministers and Men in the Far North*, p. 16.
[2] Melville's *Diary*, p. 403.   [3] Spalding, *Miscellany*, ii. p. 153.
[4] Cald., vi. p. 627.

four years the minister remained at his post, nor was his mouth closed; he was permitted to take Divine service every Sabbath morning and every Wednesday; to expound also and take public prayers every other evening of the week. In 1605 James Bischop had just come to Inverness as the regular minister; a king's man, and no friend of Bruce. Partly through his opposition, which would be all the keener because Bruce maintained separate religious services in the town, partly on account of the action of the local magistrates, Master Robert was greatly harassed during his earlier years of sojourn. One day, when Bruce was going into the fields with his two servants, a shot was fired at him out of a fisherman's cottage in the Fisher Street. The bullet missed him by only a few inches. The culprit was discovered, after long searching, hidden under the fishing-line. At his trial it came out that he was a son of the officer of old Lady Sutherland. Satisfactory guarantees were offered to Bruce, but he felt that he remained in the city only at the peril of his life.[1]

There is little evidence that the ministry thus initiated in the north bore immediate fruit. Perhaps Bruce was impatient and fretful. Out of this same house of Sutherland came some of the most happy issues of that earlier time of labour. It chanced that in the year 1606 the Earl of Sutherland and his wife and mother were confined " during the King's pleasure " at Inverness.[2] He was a nobleman with Roman Catholic leanings, and a minister had been " placed " in his home for years previous to give him instructions in the better way. Whatever prejudice there might be in the breasts of the retainers against the minister, it is clear that Bruce's teaching impressed the family themselves. The Countess Dowager was a daughter of the Catholic house of Huntly, and despite every effort of the Church she clung to the elder faith all her days.[3] The younger Countess was a kinswoman of Bruce, being of the family of Elphinstone, and she became about this time the mother of

---

[1] Cald., vii. p. 393.　　　[2] *Ibid.*, vi. p. 608.
[3] *History of the Earldom of Sutherland*, p. 409.

John, fourteenth Earl of Sutherland, who was afterwards an active opponent of the bishops, and was the first to sign the Covenant in Greyfriars Churchyard.

In the year 1611 Master John Straitoun, minister at Forres, was imprisoned in the Castle of Inverness, because he had in his teaching denounced the order of bishops, and because he refused to acknowledge the authority of the Bishop of St. Andrews.[1] Doubtless Master Robert would visit often that prisoner of Jesus Christ, and the two men would encourage one another in their God. Straitoun died in prison in the year 1613, whereupon the magistrates of Forres induced Bruce to supply the vacant pulpit for a time. The only other break to his stay at Inverness was a matter of three months, which were spent at Aberdeen.

This journey was undertaken for the sake of his health, and for the comfort of his wife and children. For at least the latter portion of this first exile his family was resident with him at Inverness. In the opening of the year 1613 he writes to his cousin, Sir James Sempill, a letter which shows how his proud spirit beat against the prison-bars. "Do not tantalise me," in effect he says, "with your vain promises of freedom. I gave them such credit that I sent home my wife and children, and spoiled myself of all my outward comforts, and exposed myself in the extremity of the season in a cold lodging in these miserable and barbarous parts, so that I have almost extinguished both my vital and sensitive spirits." He goes on to say: "His Majesty's pleasure would have been a law to me. Yea, if his Highness would command me to the scaffold, I have a good conscience to obey him, and it would be more welcome to me than this lingering death that I am in. The time has been that I have done his Majesty acceptable service, as his Highness' own handwrite beside me will bear record; which I shall leave to my posterity as their rarest jewels. . . . I am a man that has tasted of many afflictions, and I wait not who crosses me; but be it papist or atheist, bishop or minister, I will lay over all my vengeance where it belongs. . . . I pray

[1] Cald., viii. p. 160.

you, cousin, if ye delight in my conversation, let the effect declare it. . . . I will look that ye observe a Christian duty towards me. So wishing you heartily well in the Lord, I take my leave and rest, your most loving cousin to His power in God.   MR. ROBERT BRUCE.[1]

   " INNERNESSE, 10th February, 1613."

[1] Cald., vii. pp. 183, 184.

CHAPTER XVI

A Second Exile in Bruce's Old Age

In the year 1613, by the good offices of his elder son Robert, who held an appointment at Court, liberty was at length granted to the suffering servant of God to return for a space to his own house of Kinnaird. Many previous attempts had been made to remove the scandal of his detention in exile. Repeated petitions from the Assembly had been sent to the King on his behalf. The noblemen present in one Assembly wrote at the suggestion of the House, begging of his Majesty to exert his clemency in the case of Bruce. The whole process had been one of fruitless labour and evasions.

After hope had been so long deferred, liberty came at length in 1613, and continued till 1622. Though, strictly speaking, his parole confined him within the bounds of his own estate, yet he was allowed considerable scope, save that he was straitly forbidden to enter Edinburgh. It was long since he had ceased to hope for a return to his own flock. Here is a picture of what went on in St. Giles in the absence of its lawful minister: "The Bishop of St. Andrews," says James Melville, "keeps a splendid establishment in Edinburgh, consisting of his wife, children, and a great retinue of servants, and ostentatiously displays his silken robes every Sabbath in Bruce's pulpit before the magistrates and nobility."[1] Meanwhile the rightful occupant of this pulpit, "that man of God," as Calderwood says, "was tossed from place to place."

Although Bruce lacked the patronage of authority, he was consoled with a great sense of the presence of God. In the night he could not refrain from crying out at times: "I am the happiest man that ever was born, happy that ever I served

[1] *Melvini Epistolæ*, p. 125.

God." His spirit overflowed with a sense of the Divine love. On other occasions he had vexing trials to encounter, sore bodily sickness, and harassing interferences from certain ministers of the Presbytery. Bruce could never hold his peace if he saw what he considered error, whether moral or ecclesiastical. Consequently he raised up much opposition against himself. In the Presbytery of Edinburgh were now to be found men of a newer type, out of sympathy with the contendings of this faithful servant of God. They brought a charge against him, that he conducted himself like a bishop whose diocese was the whole countryside. And indeed there was a certain truth in the charge, for Robert Bruce, like John Wesley, was one of God's own episcopate; if his parish was not the world, it was the Kingdom and the whole Church. At the old pre-Reformation kirk of Cramond, which stands to this day in the kirkyard, Bruce had preached, and it was alleged that in his sermon he had called the ministers of Edinburgh false prophets. So saying, he had sounded his horn as near to the citadel as the regulations laid down for his movements would permit.[1] Next we meet him at Stirling, where he took up his residence, preaching during a vacancy in the church. But the King's missive reached him there, and he found himself restricted to Kinnaird and one mile beyond it. His teaching was in consequence limited to services in the " Gallery " of his own house. At length he purchased a permit to remove to his other dwelling of Monkland, near Glasgow, whither he travelled with his family, and where at the first he enjoyed liberty from the parish minister to preach in the church. Soon the familiar sequel occurred, and the crowd that gathered to Bruce's ministrations became so large that the Bishop of Glasgow was annoyed, and put an end to the preaching. Another cause of offence was that Bruce " kept fasts " in his own house. The reader is at once keenly interested in a complaint like this. What were the fasts which Bruce and his followers kept? It appears that a little group of about twenty persons, among them Boyd, the Principal of Glasgow University, and Scott,

[1] Cramond is but five miles distant from the city of Edinburgh.

minister in Glasgow, gathered occasionally at Bruce's mansion of Monkland for solemn services called "fasts," no doubt with a view to entreating God on behalf of their country and their Church. Another accusation was that Bruce administered the sacrament of the Supper in the Presbyterian way, disregarding the article of Perth Assembly which enacted that it should be taken on bended knees. King James found, however, that in his pursuit of these minutiæ he could not count upon the support of his own Chancellor nor of the Privy Council. So he passed the questions over to his docile Church Commission.

There is in the Advocates' Library a fragment of Bruce's Narrative,[1] from which curious and luminous details may be gleaned illustrative of his labours during the last year of his parole, namely, 1621. It was at this date, he tells us, that he repaired the ruinous Church of Larbert. "Captain William Bruce and Master William Livingstone began it, and I came in the third, after I came out of the Monkland, restoring the walls and the pulpit." Here he taught for a while, and he mentions that offence was given by his celebrating the communion in "our own Kirk of Larbert, and in Bothkennar." A new ground of offence was Bruce's venturing into Edinburgh. It chanced that Parliament was in session, so that the offence was reckoned the more grave: "coming into Edinburgh in time of Parliament to move sedition." The old man wrote a letter and made his defence also when face to face with the Privy Council, denying the charge with great spirit. Once more he produced the letter of his Majesty, wherein he acknowledged Bruce's great services to the State. His faithful wife, Martha Douglas, has lately died. She had been his guide in all business affairs, and her loss was as the loss of his right hand. He is compelled to venture personally into Edinburgh to do what formerly his wife would have done, arrange some money matters. The matter involved is 20,000 merks, and Bruce enters the city very secretly, to avoid giving any offence. His King, he says roundly before the Privy Council, has exhausted him in his living, state, and person. Let no one think that there is any

---

[1] This has been given in brief epitome in Wodrow's *Bruce*.

lust of possessions left in the heart of this aged servant of God.
When we consult the family records of Airth we find that not
long after (in 1623) Master Robert surrendered all his remaining lands to his son Robert, who was about to marry.[1]

Meantime let the eloquent pleader pursue his argument. He
was but six-and-thirty hours in Edinburgh all told. He will
account for all his movements when in the city : a call at Mr.
Alexander Merson's with reference to the marriage of his son,
a visit to David Gillespie's shop, a meeting with my Lord of
Kilsyth, who supped with him, and who is security for him in
the money transaction. He has not meddled with affairs of
Parliament; they concern him not. We seem to hear him ad-
vocating on his own behalf before the Council : " My lords and
gentlemen, I am an old man; I am weary and wasted with
grief and care, and other visitations wherewith it has pleased
the Lord in His mercy to chastise me. My servants rob me of
my possessions. Scarcely can I get any one to attend to my
wants since I have fallen under his Majesty's displeasure. It
has pleased the Lord to call upon my bed-fellow. I will tell
your lordships truly. I went out of my confine, but was driven
to it by necessity; for since God took my helper from me, I
had none to do for me. My lords, during these last five months,
while I was a prisoner in the Castle of Edinburgh, I have been
modest, calm, and peaceable.[2]

"If his Majesty will be graciously pleased to let me spend
the remnant of my aged wearisome days at my own house, I
will be glad and willing to confine myself to a limit of two
miles round about it. My lords, you will send me back to
banishment in Inverness. The hour of my journey approaches.
It is winter; the road is inhospitable and beset with dangers.
If I return to the wild north, it is not likely that I shall

---

[1] Wodrow MS., Advocates' Library, folio 42, 42.
[2] Cald., vii. pp. 509-518. Bruce was imprisoned in Edinburgh
Castle for thus venturing within the city. The picture given by the
Register of the Privy Council is one for an artist to deal with : *the
old man riding away upon the Friday early in the morning.* Mrs.
Bruce had in her possession a letter from the Bishop of Moray, permitting the minister to leave Inverness.—*Register*, ix. p. 627.

ever ——." Here occurs a flaw in the MS. which will serve us as well as words. There is a breakdown also in the heart of the writer, and his page is suffused with tears.

The pleading of Master Robert Bruce did not fail to produce an effect upon the Privy Council. Seton, the Chancellor, manfully declined, so long as he could, to "play hangman to the bishops" in their quarrel with Bruce. And the bishops themselves were not unmoved. It is told in the Narrative that at the time of the death of Bruce's wife, "the bishop suspended his persecutions for a time." On the day when Bruce was sentenced to imprisonment within Edinburgh Castle the bishops, worthy men, absented themselves, though they had brought the charge which resulted in this cruel sentence. Perhaps, like Pontius Pilate, these clergymen washed their hands of the deed, and said, "We are innocent"; but as for the King, he made no display of mercy or compunction. He blamed his Councillors for having conceded to Bruce some delay in his journey north, till the snow wreaths should thaw and the passes be open. The worm that gnawed at James' heart was envy. "We will have no more popish pilgrimages to Kinnaird," wrote the King; "he shall go to Inverness."

On the 18th of April 1622, Master Robert started upon the journey for his second term of exile. At this date he was close on seventy years of age, and long sickness and persecution had wasted his strength. Deprived as he was of the companionship of his wife, he was not forgotten of his God, who at this season sent other friends to his side. A nephew, Master James Bruce (afterwards a correspondent of Samuel Rutherford) came to visit him, escorting him upon the long, dangerous journey.[1] It must have been by Aberdeenshire that they travelled, for we are told that James Bruce came by Turriff, where David Dickson was confined, and brought back letters from him. Other friends, lay and clerical, gathered on the day of Bruce's departure, to form an escort at the start. And it is narrated that, as they mounted their horses, a vision, such as was repeatedly granted to the persecuted minister in the crises of his

[1] *Life of Robert Boyd* (Maitland Club), p. 170.

life, was wonderfully bestowed upon him. It happened that Bruce's horse was brought out last of all, and as the other riders swept past him it was observed that he paused ere he placed his foot in the stirrup, and was in a reverie, his eyes being lift up to heaven. This lasted for about a quarter of an hour, and an intimate friend, observing his attitude of devotion, drew up beside him, and, when by and by the minister mounted and rode forward he ventured to ask : " What was it you did when you fell into that muse?" The other replied : " I was receiving my commission from my Master to go to Inverness, and He gave it me Himself, before I set my foot in the stirrup, and thither I go to sow a seed in Inverness that shall not be rooted out for many ages."

On this second visit the effects of Bruce's preaching were remarkable. The first effect was keen antagonism, the Gordon clan distinguishing themselves by their opposition to the new teaching. One man there was of that great name, Sir Robert Gordon, the Tutor of Sutherland, who used the influence which he had in the north, not only in helping the Church to organise among the wild clansmen, but in the pursuit of all that was noble and good. On the other hand, Lord Enzie, eldest son of the Marquis of Huntly, otherwise known as Lord Gordon, took a dislike to Bruce, and persecuted him, even accusing him of treason, and finally driving him for a time out of Inverness altogether. The occasion of Lord Enzie's quarrel was as follows. One day there was among the worshippers in Bruce's place of meeting a certain Mr. John Gordon, minister of Stradoun, who took deep offence at the doctrine preached. Bruce had no knowledge that Gordon was in the church, but in his discourse, the topic of which was " How to cure dolours of the mind," it chanced that the preacher said : " They are unskilful physicians who would prescribe for such a disease either a drink of wine or the reading of books of romance." The particular hearer mentioned took the thrust home to himself, not for his profit, but to resent it angrily. He appealed to his chief, the Lord Enzie, with the result that Bruce found himself evicted from his lodging in Inverness, and refused quarters within the town. He took refuge in the Chanonry, ten miles farther north. By the good offices of the Lord Lovat, peace was restored.[1]

But soon other and better fruits of Bruce's preaching made themselves manifest. Some Christian people there were in the city who welcomed him back as a very apostle of Christ. Ere long a truce of God was made among the clansmen, and the chiefs, with their retainers behind them, crowded to hear the new teacher. His scheme of work was as formerly, save that now he had prayers with an exhortation every week-evening. Across the Kessock Ferry, over the breadth of the great county of Ross, from every point of the compass, they came in crowds to hear the fresh message of hope. Tradition is to this day a powerful and trustworthy medium in the Highlands by which to link the past to the present; and it is a remarkable proof of the reality of Bruce's work, that a chorus of testimonies has been handed from sire to son, to the effect that the season was one of profound awakening to concern for salvation. At the end of that same century a minister, Brand, of Bo'ness, was despatched as a deputy into the north, and he records in his Diary how he found the memory of that man of God, Robert Bruce, sweet to his day in Inverness, and he adds that multitudes of all ranks crossed the ferries to hear him. "They came from Ross and Sutherland; the Lord blessed his labours to the conversion of many." Fleming gives the same testimony. Dr. Gustavus Aird, of Creich, had spoken with Hector Home, of Invergordon, who passed on to him the confident tradition that inquirers crowded to Inverness every Sabbath over ferries and bridgeless rivers to hear Bruce.[2] The capital of the Highlands must have been in those days like Patmos, or like the jail of Philippi, glorious with the very presence of God.

One of the converts of this remarkable season was Alexander Munro, son of a laird in Kiltearn. This was the man who, being afterwards ordained to the ministry in the Reay country,

[1] Cald., vii. p. 566.
[2] *Free Church General Assembly Proceedings*, May 1888, pp. 6, 7.

was almost the first Protestant minister settled in that vast territory. It was he who translated portions of the Bible into Gaelic verse, inducing the rude people who had an ear for rhyme to commit the translations to memory. His labours were greatly owned of God. Hogg, of Kiltearn, is another name to be mentioned with reverence in connection with the Celtic revival. Some of the converts of this memorable season were alive at the date of the Revolution Settlement.

It is quite impossible to credit the statement that Bruce, who had no aptitude for learning French,[1] could, when he was well past middle life, have learnt the very difficult Gaelic tongue, in order to preach to the Highlanders. The truth is, that the inhabitants of Ross, Inverness, Cromarty, that fertile garden of the north, were in close touch through their great ports, Invergordon and Inverness, with other parts of the kingdom; and for all their savagery in some ways, they could command a broken English for commerce and common speech. And every receiver of the Word of Life would become an evangelist, so that the Highland people would proclaim from heart to heart in their own melodious Gaelic (or Irish as it was called) the amazing Divine message of pardon and peace. There is an undoubtedly authentic story which puts words into the mouth of a rough Highlander—a drover—who came into Bruce's presence after sermon to ask the way of life; and the language of which he makes use is a rude English or Scots, " I'se gie ye two coos," he said (it was all he had) " if you'll 'gree me and God."[2] These converted Highlanders became the stoutest adherents of the great covenanting movement. In 1638, just seven years after Bruce's death, the covenanters, on marching north, quite unexpectedly found their greatest successes in Inverness and in the county of Ross.[3]

Among those who visited the distinguished minister about

[1] See Chap. xii. p. 118.
[2] There are two versions of this story. I have given that of Kirkton (*History of the Church*, p. 26). Another is given by Dr. Thomas Goodwin, *Sermons*, vol. v. p. 174.
[3] Hill Burton, *History of Scotland*, vol. vi. p. 205.

this time was a young Glasgow student, Robert Blair. Blair must have been rather a coxcomb at the first, both in his bearing and in his pulpit appearances. A humble worshipper on one occasion made pointed and sarcastic reference to his extravagant style of dress;[1] and it is recorded that when the young fellow foolishly asked Bruce, who had heard him preach, what he thought of his discourse, the reply was most crushing: " I found your sermon very polished and digested, but there is one thing I miss in it—the Spirit of God."[2]

The Spirit of God—the one indispensable presence—was given richly to Bruce in his northern ministry, and among those who were drawn to visit him was Robert Blair, who must have been another sort of man by that time. Blair's friends at Glasgow, dreading what might come of Bruce's influence over him, attempted to dissuade him from the journey to Inverness, but he persisted in his determination to visit the exile. He tells that at Turriff he saw Master David Dickson, who was confined there for the sake of his faith, and by his conversation the traveller was admirably refreshed. At Inverness he found Master Robert Bruce, suffering his second exile. "That ancient heroic servant of Christ, considering how long a journey I had made from Glasgow to visit him, did impart to me the memorable passages of his life in a large book, wherein was set down what hard and sore exercise his soul had met with, as also the strong consolations whereby the Lord had comforted him."[3]

---

[1] *Select Biographies*, i. p. 340.
[2] *Autobiography of Blair*, p. vi.
[3] *Ibid.*, pp. 39, 40.

CHAPTER XVII

A Budget of Old Letters

GEORGE MEREDITH utters at least half the truth when he declares that " old letters are the dreariest ghosts in the world, and you cannot keep more treacherous rubbish in your possession." For some sorts of correspondence the only secure custody is that of the fire.

Than letters of a certain sort there can be no more spontaneous or trustworthy source of history. That Glasgow scholar, Blair, who visited Robert Bruce at Inverness, in his notes of the northern tour, speaks of choice letters written either to Bruce or by him, which the latter had copied into his large book. Perhaps that large book in the handwriting of the exile may one day be discovered. Meantime it has gone amissing. The finding of it would be better for the world than the recovery of a lost play of Shakespeare! For the present we must console ourselves with the small packet of letters that are within our reach. A few are from the pen of Bruce himself, others are from certain distinguished correspondents. In Bruce's exile, men like Andrew Melville, Principal Boyd of Trochrig, John Welsh, John Forbes were among his correspondents. Melville's letters have many a reference to his fellow-sufferer, and it must have cheered Bruce to learn of the unceasing affection of him whom he had called master. There is always an air of high courage in the words of Melville, which tends to communicate itself to his readers. False rumours had reached him in his exile at Sedan that his distinguished pupil, Bruce, together with his nephew, James Melville, was making terms with the King by submitting to the bishops. " Give my salutations to Bruce," he begs of his nephew in a letter; " tell him that I would rather

hear of his base servitude than see it."[1] This message was sent
in the year 1613, when Bruce's persecutions were abated for a
season. A certain colour was given to the suggestion that he
might yield, from the powerful influences exerted on his behalf.
Petitions were signed and many nobles and even some bishops,
and the Chancellor Seton himself, supported these; the ad-
vanced age of Bruce, his infirm health, the needs of his family
—these arguments were pressed. Certain of the sufferers for
conscience' sake allowed their opposition to be worn down by
considerations of this kind, and obtained a remission of their
sentence. But no such dreams of concession entered the mind
of the stern exile at Inverness. Melville's next letter to his
nephew indicates that he had learnt better things concerning
his friend: " I cannot but hope for everything good from Bruce.
The Court rumours are vain and calumnious, especially with
respect to heroes like him, adorned with every virtue. I am
anxious to hear good accounts of Patrick Simson, the faithful
bishop of Stirling, and a few others of the same stamp with
him."[2] In a letter to another friend, of date 1616, Andrew
Melville speaks of Bruce in terms which, however often they
have been quoted, are worthy of exact repetition. " That constant confessor," he says, " and almost martyr of our Lord
Jesus. The Lord [keep] him and his for ever. I never remember him and his without comfort, and heart lift up to God."[3]

In the intellectual revival which accompanied the Reformation, one of the most attractive of those Scottish scholars, who
brought lustre to their country and who dedicated their gifts
to the service of God, was Robert Boyd, of Trochrig. His
affection for Bruce and the closeness of their friendship in later
years make it needful that some notice be given to him in these
pages. Boyd's attachment to Bruce is at once explained when
it is said that he had been a student at Edinburgh College in
the days of Master Robert's ascendency at St. Giles. Boyd
took his degree in 1595. Many influences, he tells us, had gone
to the shaping of his life. One fellow-student, Watson, who

[1] *Melvini Epistolæ*, p. 308.   [2] *Ibid.*, p. 325.
[3] M'Crie's *Melville*, p. 487.

had lodged with him, to whom he was helpful in the study of philosophy, made him deeply his debtor in the spiritual life by his discourses, example, pattern, and fervent prayers. The influence of this fellow-student he ranked next in its effect upon him to the teaching of the incomparable Rollock (his professor), and the sermons and more private friendship of that most holy man, Master Robert Bruce (standard-bearer in true piety), whom he styles " the Basil or Bernard of our age."[1]

Influences like these led this gifted young man, son of an archbishop, to throw in his lot with the Church. He was drawn to it not so much on ecclesiastical as on religious grounds, for he found within its borders the most vital Christianity of the time. And his convictions brought him, like Bruce, into exile in France. Unlike Bruce, however, he was able with fine sympathy to enter into French life, and became a professor at Montauban where he taught at the time of Bruce's exile (1600-1), and where these kindred spirits may have met. So completely did Boyd adopt his new country that he married a French lady, and it was difficult afterwards to induce him to return to Scotland, so that his extraordinary learning was almost lost to his native country.

James VI, who prided himself on his patronage of letters, at length induced Robert Boyd to accept the principalship of Glasgow College. It was in 1614 that he returned to Glasgow, and immediately he introduced into the university such a deeply religious tone as his old Master, Principal Robert Rollock, had brought into Edinburgh University. His students could recall after thirty years the solemnity and ardour of Boyd's Latin prayers and the graciousness of his character. These are the things which young students do not readily forget.

Boyd was no controversialist, reserving the pulpit for its proper work, and having little taste for the denunciation of bishops. All the more telling, therefore, is the following passage which he wrote to Bruce while the latter was at Inverness:

[1] *Life of Robert Boyd* (Maitland Club), p. 10.

F

"May it please His merciful goodness to bring home the captivity of His dear servants, loosing their bonds, setting them again in their own stations, and yet opening their mouths to the praise of His glorious grace, whose mouths He has heretofore opened with so great a blessing towards His children, and rooting out (if not renewing and reviving them by true and humble repentance) these rotten and stinking weeds which His holy and pure hand never planted in His courts."

In this letter Boyd shows a desire to return to France, to escape the distasteful conflict which raged in Scotland. Happily for his country and his university, as well as for his friend, he remained; and some years later we learn from the journal of Boyd that Bruce visited him at Glasgow, being resident at the time in his own house of Monkland. On 22nd March 1618 the two men dined together[1] in the house of Boyd at Glasgow, and in the following year those private fasts occurred at Monkland in which both these men took a leading part.[2] Meetings of this kind were regularly kept by Boyd,—Christian Hamilton (then Lady Boyd), Margaret Livingstone, Master Robert Scott, minister of Glasgow, and Robert Bruce frequenting them. Conventicles of this kind were anathema to the bishops. "I hear," writes Lady Boyd to Trochrig, the Principal, in the year 1621—"I hear that there is some appearance of your getting into trouble by reason that the King, his Majesty, is displeased with you for your being with Master Robert Bruce."[3]

It was the custom of those who suffered for the testimony of Jesus to encourage each other, if possible, by meeting together for prayer, otherwise by brotherly correspondence. Several letters are in our hands which were addressed to Bruce with this note of appeal. Here is the cry of one prisoner of Jesus Christ, Charles Ferme, who was confined in the island of Bute about 1608. "I have to this hour been relieved by the comfort

---

[1] *Life of Robert Boyd* (Maitland Club), ii. p. 135.
[2] Fragment of Bruce's Narrative, epitomised by Wodrow (*Bruce*, p. 128). Wodrow MSS., Advocates' Library, Folio 42, 42.
[3] *Ladies of the Covenant*, p. 17.

of no creature; neither have I here to whom I may go. A thousand deaths hath my soul tasted of; but still the mercy and truth of the Lord hath succoured me. The Lord perfect His own work in me."[1]

This Ferme, or Farholme, as he was otherwise called, had a connection of long standing with Bruce. He was a regent in the college of Edinburgh, and it must have been when engaged lecturing to the students that (12th September 1598) he was sought for by the session of the Church of St. Giles to preach there " at such times and necessary occasions as he shall be employed by the session." In other words, Ferme was invited at that time to be Bruce's assistant.[2] He appears next in history as minister of Fraserburgh. Like so many of the Presbyterians of the time, he was a scholar, and it was sorry evidence of James VI's support of learning that he should send this gifted minister " into the Highlands for the Assembly holden at Aberdeen." Ferme's touching letter found Bruce at Inverness, a fellow-sufferer able doubtless to minister the needed word of comfort, which would be " returned seven-fold to his own bosom."

Two other correspondents of the exile, Bruce, must be named, those fellow-prisoners of the " foul hole " of Blackness Castle, John Forbes and John Welsh. Forbes was a son of the laird of Corse, Aberdeenshire. Though his brother, Patrick, the famous and godly Bishop of Aberdeen, acquiesced in King James' ecclesiastical policy, this John Forbes was of other stuff, and took up a position of strong antagonism. As moderator of that Aberdeen Assembly of 1605 which met without royal authority, and even in the face of a royal prohibition, he was a special object of attack. The offence was called treason, forasmuch as the ministers denied that James had any control over an action which was purely ecclesiastical. They stood for the liberties of the Church. The speech of Forbes in his defence was exceedingly eloquent, but despite the justice of their cause and the weight of their pleading, the five ministers who were impeached were brought in guilty by a packed jury,

[1] Cald., vi. p. 702.   [2] M'Crie's *Melville*, p. 377, n.

and they were sent to Blackness Castle. After fourteen months of solitary confinement in his dungeon Forbes was banished to France.

The letter of Forbes to Bruce extends to nearly five pages, and is a long vindication of his own conduct in a delicate affair which concerned the Chancellor Seton. Commonly, it is alleged that the leaders of our Scottish Church in the seventeenth century were lacking in the grace of charity. No doubt, charity was not so much their gift as that equally noble virtue, dogged tenacity of purpose. If there is more of the one grace, there is certainly less of the other to-day; and while we point out the defects of our ancestors, let us admire their great qualities also. The matter of Forbes and Seton, the Chancellor, exhibits a rare and exquisitely delicate instance of charity, such as might bring glory to any age. The letter in question is dated Edinburgh Castle. Welsh and Forbes had been brought thither from Blackness for the purpose of giving evidence in a charge which had been made against the Chancellor. It must be kept in mind that Seton had given his vote as president only a few months before to send Forbes and his brethren to prison. And now the tables were turned, and Forbes had possession of information which would ruin Seton with the King, and deprive him of his office. To the amazement of all, he refused to give the evidence, and would neither be coaxed nor browbeaten into a disclosure. It is pleasing to have to add that the Chancellor was cleared, and retained his office.

Master John details this curious and tangled affair in his letter, passing on to some melancholy reflections about " unsatiable hatred " and " malicious hunting of lives of the innocent." " Other things," he concludes, " I refer to my brother Master John Welsh's letter, beseeching you to support our weakness under our burthen with your prayers for us, as we shall remember you to God daily. For as in the heaven we have none but Him, so in the earth there is none with Him. To His grace and consolation I most heartily commend you, remembering my loving salutation to your bed-fellow.—Your loving brother in the Lord, and fellow-sufferer in His truth,

"JOHN FORBESSE.

"EDINBURGH CASTLE, 16th July 1606."

Master John Welsh, who wrote to Bruce at the same time from the prison of Edinburgh, was, like Forbes, the son of a Scottish laird, and he married a daughter of John Knox. The prowess of Mrs. Welsh in defence of those principles for which her father and her husband suffered is well known, and the story of her bold bearing in the presence of King James is one of those classics which need no re-telling. Welsh like Forbes, took refuge in France.[1] There is a letter from him to Bruce, dated St. Joan, 20th (Nov.) 1619. It was sent home by the hands of a young nephew of the latter, a student in French colleges, and it would reach his correspondent during the interval between his two northern exiles:—

"RIGHT REVEREND AND DEARLY BELOVED BROTHER,—I would not let this occasion pass to write you by the bearer, your kinsman, whose comportment in this country hath always been with honour, giving testimonies of true religion and godliness in the places of his sojourn, which for some time was with me. The *Nullitie of the Assemblie at Perth*, being sent to me, hath taken all pretext of ignorance and excuses away, and I judge them blessed who in a desertion so universal keep their garments clean without spot. Of the which, sir, ye are one whose testimony to the truth and against the defection brought in is known to all the churches. The persecution is lamentable, but without all question when the chaff is discovered, He will not let the rod of the wicked remain for ever upon the back of the righteous. It is no marvel if after so long a peace, so great a liberty, and the enjoyment of the gospel in such abundance, at last He send the fiery trial. What my mind is concerning the root of these branches, the bearer will show you more fully. They are no more to be accounted orthodox, but apostates, . . . and therefore not to be heard any more,

[1] See pp. 118-119.

neither in public nor in consistories, colleges nor synods. For what fellowship hath light with darkness? So with the measure the Lord hath given, I recommend you to His sufficient grace, and your whole family.—Your loving brother, and unworthy to be called the servant of Christ,

"MR. JOHNE WELSHE."[1]

Of those letters from Bruce's own pen, which are still within our reach, some are controversial, others are more devotional. We have already had samples of the one kind; the other kind, of which, too few, alas, remain, must have gone broadcast over the religious world, both in Scotland and England and in the Continent. The samples which remain, reminding us in some ways of Samuel Rutherford's letters, only deepen our regret that most of Bruce's correspondence is irrecoverable. One author who wrote eight years after Bruce's death actually placed in the same MS. volume letters of Rutherford and Bruce, with the tantalising remark that other letters of Bruce were to be seen.[2] Many of these must have been addressed to women, such as the Lady Culross, the Lady Eglinton, or the Lady Kilsyth, whose own correspondence shows a close association with Master Robert and his circle. It was as a pastor skilled in the cure of souls that Bruce wrote his most remarkable letters, and he was sought after by conscience-stricken, sin-laden folk in their quest for relief. There was one striking instance, that of Mrs. Drake, and as one reads in the pages of Quick's *Icones* her "doleful case," one is reminded of Bunyan's "Badman" or the *Holy War*. Mrs. Drake was for ten years burdened under a dismal despair, fearing that she should be reprobate. Some wise friend of the distressed lady sought the help of Bruce, and he prayed on her behalf, and interposed otherwise with so happy a result that the sufferer found peace. Bruce burst into prophecy in ecstatic assurance of her final salvation, and in the following fashion he apostrophised the adversary of her soul:—

[1] Cald., vii. pp. 409, 410.
[2] Wodrow's *Life of Robert Bruce*, pp. 139, 140.

" O enemy, Satan! although thy enmity for the present be troublesome unto this patient, yet I thank my God through Jesus Christ that thou art an enemy unto her, and that He hath put her in His camp to fight against thee. When I consider how in Paradise the Lord proclaimed irreconcilable enmity betwixt thee and the blessed Seed, I account her happy in that thou art her enemy, and that strength is given her to fight against thee. For hereby I perceive she is none of thine, but stands on that side whereof Christ is the Captain, and all the saints are soldiers, where the victory undoubtedly must be both sure and certain on her side. O deceitful serpent, if we find such terrors and ensigns of thy fury for these smaller sins of frailty, which we foolishly by thy enticement commit, what should we have found if we had followed thee in the rest of thy deadly insidious and immeasurable fiery injected temptations, from the which the Lord's preventing and restraining mercy hath kept us? I have often by experience heard that thou art a faithless traitor, because thou temptest a man to sin, and for the self-same sin which by thy instigation we commit thou art the first accuser and the last tormentor. The Lord increase our faith and confirm His good purpose in our hearts, that we never hearken any more to thy lying words, nor suffer our souls to be circumvented by thee and thy deceitful snares. And as for the work of her salvation, since it is a work which our God will work in spite of thee, wherefore should she or we any more regard thy lying testimony? Thou didst most maliciously put the question unto our Saviour, whether or no He were the Son of God. And then what marvel is it that thou darest say unto His children that they are none of His? Is there any such undoubted truth that thou darest not deny? or any falsehood which thou darest not make good and justify? Why, therefore, should we enter into disputing with thee? For her salvation consists not either in thy questioning nor in her disputing against it, but upon the Lord's unchangeable decree of election. If thou shouldst speak for her, and plead her cause, she were so much the worse. I love no testimony which proceeds from thee. When thou confessedst that Jesus was the Son of God, He rebuked thee, and would have none of thy testimony; and when thou cryedst out that Paul and Silas were the servants of the most High God, although thou spakest the truth, yet they would not accept of thy testimony. So, although thou wouldst affirm that she were the child of God, were she anything the better? Nay, but so much the worse. Thou canst vent no truth but with an intent to deceive. Therefore keep thy testimony to thyself. Speak what thou wilt, thou art ever, like thyself, a liar. Cursed art thou, and cursed shalt thou be with all thy confederates, and cursed are they that are in friendship with thee! So in conclusion, thy pursuit of her, and her safety hitherto from thy power, shows me that she is none of thine.

"The Lord pour in His comfort and grace in her weak heart! that she may find and feel the sweetness of the things we write of, and from her feeling to give God the praise of His glory and of her victory, which I am sure to be most certain in God's good time, and that her salvation is as sure as mine own, I praise God."[1]

There are two letters of the year 1629, two years before the death of Bruce, the interest of which lies chiefly in their disclosure of a chastened, mellow spirit, as of one who had taken joyously the spoiling of his goods. Throughout the vicissitudes of exile, that leal heart clung constant to the flock in Edinburgh on whom he had bestowed his prime, and who had stood by him in the midst of good or evil report. In the first letter, of date 20th January 1629, entitled " A letter written by that faithful servant of God, Master Robert Bruce, to a friend, after he was deposed from his ministry in Edinburgh," there are references to the city which had cast him out, and it is plain to the reader that the heart of the old man has gone back over a quarter of a century to the fruitful pastorate of St. Giles. Evidently the King (now no more the unreliable James, but his son Charles I) had given him leave to enter Edinburgh town occasionally, but solely for Sabbath preach-

[1] Quick's *Icones Sacræ Anglicanæ*, Dr. Williams' London Library (Transcript), pp. 183-185.

ing. The most attractive picture in this letter, of which the author begs his readers to excuse the length (but we will hardly grumble over that), is the old master himself, an adept in the art of self-abnegation, reading his book, or kneeling at his prayers, his only complaint being that his will is "not so bent as it should have been neither." The page is characteristically suffused with tears; and the "hearing of voices" in the day time, and the audible testifying of the Spirit to his spirit for his encouragement, will not cause surprise to those who are initiated in the ways of God with His confiding children.

"KINNAIRD, *the 20th of January* 1629,—Brother, my heart: I write unto thee to prepare thee in good earnest and with a good heart lifted up and poured out upon God in Christ. Take pains, my heart, great pains, inward and secret pains; nothing is won without great diligence. My enemies, the worst that they can do, the Lord has turned into the best. I never got such access in my time as I have gotten since I went from you. The treasures of His riches have been opened unto me. There was never such foul flesh has gotten a more gracious, more sensible, more powerful approbation of my ministry in Edinburgh, of my fidelity therein. His Spirit has testified to my spirit, not only by real joys, spiritual and elevated light, but by vocal speeches within me in the daylight, that I heard so sensibly with great effusion of tears, so far not only by approbation, but to my commendation, that I admire how He should bestow such gracious speeches upon so wretched creature as I was. Indeed, I grant the will was with me, but not so bent as it should have been neither, for I was over timorous, and laden with diversity of infirmities; the spirit in some measure ready, but the flesh was weak. Yet His Majesty, my gracious God, my God in Christ, accepts of it, as it had been the most perfect and exact service in the world: yea, I admire how so true a mouth could speak so far in approbation of a silly poor wretch. My heart, howsoever Edinburgh has cast me off, rejected and banished me out of their parts, I leapt no sooner on my horse, but the gates of heaven were cast open to me;

I got such applause in my heart, with such floods of tears, with such real and constant approbation, that my heart could not wish for greater access. And on the second day of the same month I got another approbation in distinct terms, the Spirit testifying to my spirit so audibly (as it were), that I admired how His Majesty could make so much of so little doings, and so mean service; and surely I cannot say that ever that day goes over my head wherein I get not a sign and a sense of His comfortable presence. I got two within the town also very significantly. M. C. came, in the middle of the first of them, in my own chamber. I was reading indeed, and on my meditation. And so, my heart, although man has left me, and namely your ministry, yet my sweet Lord has not left me. I never forgathered with a better Master; I never got a sweeter fee and better wages, and I look for a very rich reward. So ye have cause not only to pray, but to praise God greatly for me; that He is so bountiful, and that He meets me above my very expectation. There comes never a thing to me, trouble or alteration, but he gives me warning before, mollifying my heart so notably, and giving me such tears of joy, that I am ever ashamed of myself, that I cannot be thankful. Alwise I get out these words to you all, and namely to your sisters that gave me such signs of reverence, that my God remains my God in a copious manner; that there is a great curse upon Edinburgh, and namely upon the ministry and magistracy, be learned as they will, and count themselves so. I will assure you, as far as I have learned, they are not taught of God, nor sent in mercy by His Holy Spirit unto you; and I am content this writing be plain, to testify my censure. They have gone about to make me odious to his Majesty (the King) and to all honest men. But indeed I shall not meet them so. It is long since my Lord Ochiltree wrote to his lady, or she wrote out of your town that he studied to disgrace me at his Majesty's hands. And then they could not get him persuaded; but now he has written to the Council with his own letter. I never came to Edinburgh but upon a charge of the Lord's letter, and taught on the Sabbath to sanctify the Sabbath, and to hold

in my gift. And this cannot be a crime, because it is warranted both by God and the King. Alwise, for it I am shut out, and made incapable of mutual consolation.

"This letter is longer than becomes me, but it is an ease to my mind; yea, I beseech God to teach me, as He has done those twenty days bygone, by sweet seals. Now to these sweet seals I commend you, Andrew Hart's wife, Elizabeth Michelson, Elizabeth Craig, and all the rest of them that have the mark of Christ in their forehead, with my pastoral blessing; and so rests your loving pastor in Christ.—MR. ROBERT BRUCE."[1]

It will be admitted by every reader that there is a good strain of the natural man in this letter; and in that also which follows, the occasion of which is the publication of some pasquil or satire wherein Master Robert has been jeered at as "ignorant." The spirit of the old lion in his lair leaps out to reply, and expressions like "debauched sycophant" show how deeply he has been moved. My Lord Ochiltree's slander of Bruce to the King still rankles, but that noble recollection of his conversion more than fifty years before in the Castle of Airth overshadows every other memory:—

"As for him that made that pasquil, I know him not. Alwise for his objection of 'ignorance,' I take with it, and do confess the same. Surely I may say both wholly and truly that I have taken pains to banish it for these fifty years; and I may say justly, that I have been a continual student; and I hope I may say it without offence, that he is not within the Isle of Britain of my age that takes greater pains upon his Bible. I must leave the blessing to the great God. . . . Indeed, the time has been when it pleased His Divine Majesty to open mine eyes and to present my whole sins unto me, and let me see time and place and person, to cast me down terribly, and then to pour in after this His redolent balm on the bleeding wounds of a festered conscience; and to make me to know myself, that my sins were forgiven me—to know by senses and to know by

[1] Wodrow's *Life of Bruce*, pp. 134-136.

perfect feeling, to know by experience and by experimental knowledge; and except I would lie, I do not lack both now and then, documents from His own Spirit speaking to my spirit, that He counts better of me and my labours than they are worthy. But He doth it in rich mercy, and happy am I that I entered to serve Him, and sorry am I that I cannot mend my hand; and glad would I be (He knows) to do the thing that might honour Him, that might procure my credit, advance my credit or keep my credit at His glorious hand; and through the merit of Christ . . . I look in His mercy to my last breath to grow in credit and to keep my credit with His Divine Majesty; and that by renewing my daily repentance, to live and die a penitent sinner."[1]

This letter is dated Kinnaird, 30th March 1629. That which follows, dated Kinnaird, 2nd September 1629, is of peculiar interest as the latest writing of Bruce which has yet been recovered.[2] The familiar signature is in a very trembling hand, but all who read these lines must feel that Bruce's intrepid spirit is in nowise quenched. His correspondent is the Lady Eglinton, wife of " the pious Eglinton " Alexander, the sixth earl. This Lord Eglinton stands out as a friend of Master David Dickson, the minister of Irvine. And no leal Scottish heart can forget how, on Dickson's suffering sentence of banishment (the bishop addressing him in Court " as if he had been speaking to a dog "), Lord Eglinton befriended him, sheltered him in his own castle, and caused him teach in the Hall weekly, in defiance of the judgment.[3] The Countess was as true a friend as her husband to the cause of the persecuted Church. In her youth, as Lady Anna Livingstone, she had been a maid-of-honour to James Sixth's queen, and was married in 1612. Wodrow tells a good story concerning her.[4] One day David Dickson came in to see this great dame when she had with her the Ladies Culross and Wigton, all of them true

---

[1] Wodrow's *Bruce*, pp. 137, 138.
[2] It will be found, printed with all the quaint archaic forms of spelling, in *Memorials of the Montgomeries*, vol. i. p. 223.
[3] Cald., vii. pp. 540, 541.   [4] *Analecta*, i. 19.

"Ladies of the Covenant." "They all caressed the good minister very much, till he said: 'Ladies, if all this kindness be to me as Master David Dickson, I owe you no thanks; but if it be to me as a servant of my Master's and for His sake, I take it all well.'"

The Countess of Eglinton seems to have been suffering from some domestic trouble, in connection with which Master Robert Bruce ministers consolation:—

"MADAM,—I cannot tell at what school your Ladyship has been, but surely your Ladyship's last letter savoured of grace, had a fragrant perfume of the doctrine of the Holy Spirit. I see your Ladyship's cross is sanctified. I fear ye had need of patience, that after ye have done His will, ye may report His promise. There is nothing that assures me more of your election. Suppose ye be unequally yoked, it is for your good and for your humiliation; for your Ladyship is sent to your prayer to be very earnest that the eyes of the instrument that exercises your Ladyship may be illuminated, and the person sanctified, whether it be he or she; that they may become a sweet and gracious comfort to you. And in the meantime, the Lord strengthens your Ladyship that He lay no more on your Ladyship than He gives you strength to bear. Indeed, it knits my heart unto your Ladyship, for I see clearly the Lord has appointed you to be a vessel of honour. This is the cross of Christ that is upon your Ladyship, and it will sanctify the domestic. I never found your Ladyship so redolent. If I were near you I would gar you smell more, in my mind; but, as it is, ye shall have my entire affection, with my humble intercession that my sweet Lord may supply my want, and not only do your Ladyship good, but all that are in your case. Ye would be a formal Christian, Madam, if ye wanted that; a painted sepulchre, an outward professor. But now that ye endure, the force of religion is at your heart. And now ye must wait on, till He that has laid it on, of His sweetest mercies, take it off, and raise you up comforts of your children and of some of your brethren, and others about you, to strengthen your Ladyship's inward man that he faint not and that he grow not weary. I have written to Master David (Dickson), your neighbour, myself [no doubt asking him to visit the Countess], and so I will end with regard to your Ladyship's troubles. So, with my best affections, for indeed, Madam, I would gladly take a part of your Ladyship's burden off you; and that which I cannot do I will commend it to One who will do it indeed, as I see He doeth it already.

"To whose sweetest mercies I commend your Ladyship, children and all, and so rests, Your Ladyship's most loving cousin and faithful friend,

 [1]

NOTE TO CHAPTER XVII

The case of Mrs. Joan Drake, wife of Francis Drake of Amersham, has been narrated by the Rev. John Hart in his book, *Trodden Down Strength, by the God of Strength, or Mrs. Drake Revived*, 1647. It was as notorious a case of conscience as that of Francis Spira, though the issue was happier. It appears that many skilled physicians of the soul dealt with this sufferer; Dr. Usher, afterwards Primate of Ireland, Thomas Hooker, and Mr. John Dod, of Ashby, being among these. Master Robert Bruce, "some time minister in Edinburgh," wrote his letter to Mrs. Drake somewhere about the time of his first exile in the north. As the title of Hart's book indicates, the suffering of the lady was followed by an exceeding great joy and assurance in Christ, in the possession of which she died. Those who cannot consult the Rev. John Hart's inter-

---

[1] There is no "Master" prefixed to this, Bruce's latest known autograph, though in previous letters the prefix regularly occurred.

esting narrative in the British Museum can study a brief account of Mrs. Joan Drake contained in *Memoirs of Pious Women,* by Samuel Burden (1815), vol. ii., pp. 1-22. Can this John Hart be the I. H. who edited " *The Way to True Peace and Rest,* XVI. Sermons of Mr. Robert Bruce, London, 1617 "?

CHAPTER XVIII

Christ is in Life and in Death Advantage

THE sojourn of Master Robert at Inverness resulted in the forming of other ties besides, which were only less precious than those of the religious life. Elizabeth Bruce, his elder daughter, became engaged to the son and heir of the Commissary of Inverness. The name of this young man was James Campbell, younger of Moy, near Forres.[1] In September 1624, Master Robert Bruce obtained leave to travel south for the marriage. The time limit of this concession was ultimately extended, as the winter season had come; and in March 1625, by the stern arbitrament of death, his penalty was mitigated. James the Sixth was gone to his account, and King Charles did not insist on the exile, but permitted the aged minister for the short remainder of his days to dwell in his own house at Kinnaird.

During those six last years of Master Robert's life he underwent a sort of apotheosis while he was yet alive. The only valid canonisation is that which is obtained at the hands of Christ's own followers, who recognise and do homage to sanctity as to no other Christian grace. Larbert Church became the Mecca of many pilgrimages. While Bruce, however, conducted services in that pre-Reformation building which he had repaired at his own charges, it is pathetic to find that still he doggedly regarded himself as minister of St. Giles, Edinburgh. "There is not now a lawful minister of Edinburgh living except I; for they have all entered in a corrupt way," he wrote so late as 1629.[2] Debarred, however, from preaching there any more, he found that his Master gave him all Scot-

---

[1] *The Bruces of Airth*, by W. Bruce Armstrong, p. 82.
[2] Row's *History of the Kirk*, p. 347.

land for his charge, and that in country houses, in open-air meetings, or in churches where the ministers invited him, great conventicles of people ever hung eager upon his message. The group of well-known " ladies of the Covenant," women of ripe Christian character and often of high social position, gathered around him, calling him master. A knot of young men also, the most promising of the new generation, drew to him, that they might learn from his lips the more perfect way. It is always a chief test of the quality of an old man when the younger men come round about him, forming a school. What influence was it that attracted so many of the younger ministers toward Bruce, so that they were willing to sit at his feet? It was that combination of unworldliness and passionate idealism which is the mark of the mystic and the saint, conferring on human life a majesty always. No one is so quick to estimate motives and to gauge ideals as a young man; no one is quite so ready to censure—or to idealise. And it is a convincing proof that Master Robert Bruce cast a spell over the Church, when we find the very choicest young ministers of the newer time hailing him as their guide—Alexander Henderson, John Livingstone, Robert Blair, and many besides.

Alexander Henderson became the leader of the Church in what is known as the Second Reformation. The story, therefore, of his conversion by means of a sermon which Bruce preached in a church not far from Leuchars, Henderson's parish, has a peculiar value, for it exhibits Bruce as the medium by which the torch was passed on from Knox's hand (whom he met in his youth at St. Andrews in 1571) to Henderson, whom he influenced in his old age.[1] It is, of course, well known that Henderson, in the beginning of his ministry, was of the Prelatic party, and that he was thrust into the charge of Leuchars against the will of the people, who locked the church doors to prevent his intrusion. His supporters made their way inside by breaking open a window. Soon afterwards the lately settled minister was induced from curiosity to attend

[1] This incident is narrated by various contemporary authors. For full details, see Wodrow's *Correspondence*, vol. iii. p. 30.

a communion service conducted by Bruce in the church of Forgan,[1] adjoining his own parish. He crept into a dark corner under one of the galleries. Bruce entered the pulpit, majestic and calm, and after a pause, as was his manner, he read with great deliberateness from St. John x. 1, words singularly apt to the case of one lurking hearer: " He that entereth not by the door into the sheepfold, but climbeth up some other way, is a thief and a robber." It was from this text that many years before, in the High Church of Glasgow, Principal Smeaton had protested against the forcing of Robert Montgomery, loaded with his " enormous crimes," upon the city as its archbishop.[2] Bruce may have had the historic use of the verse in his mind when he gave out his text. It is probable that the solemn scripture, thus gravely declaimed, would suggest to Henderson, who was a scholar of Church History, that peculiar train of reflection which produced so happy an issue. It is certain that the words, whether chosen deliberately to meet Henderson's case or not, went like drawn swords to his conscience. That day he reckoned the day of his conversion, and he called Bruce his father in Christ. The date of this incident can be fixed as about 1615.[3]

Something must be now told concerning Master Robert's influence over that extraordinary figure of the new religious revival, John Livingstone. This young minister was a devoted listener and student at Larbert in 1627, and his testimony is invaluable: " No man in his time spake with such evidence and power of the Spirit: no man had so many seals of conversion: yea, many of his hearers thought no man since the apostles spoke with such power." There are some

---

[1] Dr. Hay Fleming says it was Forgan (Guide to St. Andrews, p. 125), and he kindly informs me that he had the information in 1877 from a gentleman, now dead, who had used the very pew (and his uncle before him). There was a confident tradition in the family that theirs was the pew in which Henderson had sat. The uncle had obtained permission to make a window in the church, so that he might be able to read his Bible. Dr. Hay Fleming accepts the tradition, and it is given above on his great authority.

[2] Spottiswood, History, p. 319.

[3] Robert Bruce's Sermons, by Rev. John Laidlaw, D.D., pp. lx. lxi.

special occasions during those closing years when we vainly wish that we could have been present; that season in the Old Church of Larbert when the preacher lingered so long on his knees in the vestry that a messenger was sent to call him out to preach; or that tryst in Andrew Ainslie's house, Edinburgh, when John Livingstone with a fellow-student, the Tutor of Bonnington, came in to have speech with Bruce. Like St. Andrew with St. Peter, Livingstone would bring his comrade into the presence of the man who had made Christ more real to him. It was eight in the morning when those eager young seekers knocked at Bruce's door, and the old man was still in bed. " He said to us, you must go and leave me for some time. I thought yesternight when I lay down that I had a good measure of the Lord's presence : and now I have wrestled (in prayer) this hour or two, and have not yet got access."[1] It must have been from the example of Bruce that these young men learnt how to pray. The Tutor of Bonnington, whose name was William Cunningham, spent ordinarily the most part of every forenoon in prayer, Bible-reading, and meditation. There is a good story of his visiting a certain man in prison under sentence of death, which shows that he was an apt disciple of Bruce in devotion to duty as well as in the cultivation of the inward life.

Once more, we might long to have been of that select company who met with Master Robert at his house of Kinnaird in 1631, just two months before he departed. John Livingstone was of the party, and so also was the Lady Culross, who mentions the occasion in a letter; but the table-talk, the Christian fellowship, fragrant with the odours of Paradise, is not on record.[2]

It is apparent that Bruce's visits, in the years 1625 to 1631, to the homes of godly folk throughout the land, and the gathering of kindred spirits to his hearth at Kinnaird or to his Larbert church, were the means of a great quickening in the

---

[1] Livingstone's "Memorable Characteristics," *Select Biographies*, i. pp. 306, 307, 341.
[2] See Letter of Lady Culross, *Select Biographies*, i. pp. 359, 360.

religious life. Those days of his preaching were days of the Son of Man. Here is a picture to look well upon. It is taken from a letter dated 1627 by Lady Margaret Livingstone, wherein is described a visit of Master Robert Bruce to the great house of Cumbernauld: " I will entreat your Ladyship to have me excused for not writing, in respect of Master Robert Bruce being here, whom I mind to keep still with me till your Ladyship's coming. He teaches to my lady this forenoon, and there are to hear him the Ladies Boyd and Kilsyth, with Kilsyth himself."[1]

Two of these " honourable women," who figure prominent in the new movement of the Covenants, were the means in God's hand of that revival at the Kirk of Shotts which took place on 21st June 1630. Let the memorable story be told once again, and repeated to our children, that God may have glory. At Shotts, a parish midway between Glasgow and Edinburgh, high up on the moorland, there lived a good minister, John Home, who had spent his life in that place. He was very poor. He lived in a miserably uncomfortable house by the wayside. But this minister was wont to bid the very best men whom he could secure for a communion season, and the Table of the Lord was sumptuously spread at the Kirk of Shotts. It chanced that one day the Marchioness of Hamilton was driving past that way, and her Ladyship's carriage broke down on the road. This accident led to the lady taking shelter under the roof of Master John Home, who with Katharine his good wife made her welcome. In return for this kindness the Marchioness, observing that the manse was most uncomfortable and even ruinous, had a new house built for the minister and his wife and family. In acknowledgment of her generosity, Mr. Home asked if he could make any return. Lady Hamilton requested that at the approaching communion season certain ministers, whom her influence could secure, might be invited to take part in the solemnity at Kirk of Shotts. The occasion must have formed a memorable " house-heating " for the newly built manse, when guests like Robert Bruce, David

[1] *Memorials of the Montgomeries*, vol. i. p. 218.

Dickson, Robert Blair, and young John Livingstone[1] were present. It was a season, too, not soon forgotten at the church, for prayers and exhortations were maintained during some five days almost without intermission. Master Robert preached with all his wonted majesty and authority, and administered the sacrament. By this date he was seventy-five years of age. The other ministers shared also in the work.

Livingstone tells how the table services were so full of awe and divine power that the people would not go away. Lady Culross offered her room for an all-night prayer service, her own supplications for the outflow of the Divine Spirit being unusually fervent. It was decided to hold a Monday thanksgiving, a custom which was not in those days observed, and when the minister to whom the conduct of the Monday service had been assigned, happened to become unwell, Lady Culross suggested that young John Livingstone should be asked to preach. Livingstone had conducted service in the Kirk of Shotts several times previously, but he was most reluctant to stand up on that Monday before so great a company, among whom were folk of high rank, and others of ripe Christian experience. He tells that, wandering out among the fields early in the morning, he seriously thought of stealing away to escape the ordeal. But God was making ready by this apparently fortuitous conjunction of events to manifest forth His glory. We cannot help wondering why the word was not given that day by the lips of venerable Master Robert Bruce, or of good Master John Home, the pastor. It is the method of God's Spirit to find new and unexpected instruments, as was the case at Stewarton, when David Dickson, of Irvine, brought revival to the church of a neighbour, or as at Dundee, when the Rev. William Burns reaped where M'Cheyne had sown.

The multitude who were drawn together on that Monday became so great that, as was not unusual in those times of revived religious interest, the church could not hold them all, and it was decided to meet in the churchyard. A trustworthy tradition points to the western end of the kirkyard as the spot

[1] See Blair's *Autobiography*, p. 90.

where Livingstone stood. His text is before us, " Then will I sprinkle clean water upon you, and ye shall be clean : a new heart also will I give you, and a new spirit will I put within you " (Ezek. xxxvi. 25, 26). He himself speaks of the liberty and melting of heart which came over him, " the like of which I never had before in public in all my life." Another account tells how a soft rain began to fall, and when the people sought for shelter the preacher broke out into an exhortation : " What a mercy it is that the Lord sifts that rain through these heavens on us, and does not rain down fire and brimstone as He did on Sodom." So he exhorted the people to flee from impending wrath. Whereupon there fell a plenteous rain from heaven, even the power of the promised Spirit, as on the day of Pentecost. Near five hundred, says a trustworthy witness, had a discernible change wrought on them, of whom the most proved living Christians afterwards.[1] It was the longest day of the year, 21st June 1630. How the Christian heart prays for such another benediction! We would fain cry out in the words of Joshua upon his date of victory: " Sun, stand thou still in Gibeon; and thou, Moon, in the valley of Ajalon."

To this day of revival at the Kirk of Shotts must be traced the springs of that Covenanting testimony which was given during the generation that followed. Eight years later, when the Covenants were sealed, it was found that the strength of the movement lay in the middle ward of the county of Lanark, wherein stands, embosomed upon the moorland, the Kirk of the parish of Shotts and the celebrated kirkyard.

Surely the venerable minister, Robert Bruce, sang that day his " Nunc dimittis " after the manner of " just and devout old Simeon." For he would recognise that God had given him an answer to his prayers, and that He had not forsaken His land.

Livingstone narrates many dramatic incidents that cast light upon the closing years of Bruce's life. Four years before the end, the old man, now more than three-score and ten, longed

---

[1] Wodrow's *Select Biographies*, i. p. 138; Wodrow's *Analecta*, i. p. 271; Gillies, *Historical Collections*, i. pp. 308-310.

to depart. "I wonder," said he, "why I am kept here so long; I have now lived two years in violence,"—by which he meant that his life had stretched two years beyond the allotted span.

The close was very gentle, being wholly without pain or sickness. Bruce came down to breakfast on the very morning of his death. His younger daughter, Martha, was by his side, and he enjoyed the morning meal. As he mused in silence, suddenly he cried: "Hold, daughter, hold; my Master calleth me." He asked that the Bible should be brought, the large house Bible,[1] but his sight failed him, and he could not read. "Cast me up the 8th of Romans," cried he, and he repeated much of the latter portion of this scripture, till he came to the last two verses, "I am persuaded, that neither death, nor life, nor angels, nor principalities, nor powers, nor things present, nor things to come, nor height, nor depth, nor any other creature, shall be able to separate us from the love of God, which is in Christ Jesus our Lord." "Set my finger on these words," said the blind, dying man: "God be with you, my children. I have breakfasted with you, and shall sup with my Lord Jesus this night. I die believing in these words."[2] The scene reminds one of that last episode of the deathbed of Knox, when he turned to his wife and said: "Go read to me where first I cast anchor." It is well for a man to have some sure word of scripture by which he can live, and in the faith of which he may find it easier to die.

So Master Robert Bruce departed this life upon 27th July 1631. An immense concourse of between four thousand and five thousand mourners of all ranks assembled to the funeral. In accordance with a wish expressed by him in his lifetime, no memorial sermon was preached. The grave was dug within the precincts of the ancient church, at the very foot of the

---

[1] This Bible is still in the hands of representatives of the family. There are notes in the margin in Bruce's hand, as well as entries of the names of descendants. See p. 184.

[2] Fleming, *Fulfilling of Scripture*, i. p. 379; *Select Biographies*, i. p. 308.

pulpit which Bruce's piety had restored. A modern church
has taken the place of the old pre-Reformation edifice, and
reverent hands have reared a modern tombstone to com-
memorate the great Reformer. But within there has been
carefully preserved that old flat gravestone which was Bruce's
original memorial. Its Latin inscription, signifying "Christ in
life and in death is gain," contains in it the secret of Master
Robert Bruce's career.

NOTE TO CHAPTER XVIII

The Latin words carved upon Robert Bruce's grave,
" *Cristus in vita et in morte lucrum,*" are from Beza's version
of Philip. i. 21. Upon this version the English version of the
Geneva Bible was founded, as appears, *e.g.*, from the rendering of the text in question : " For Christ is to me both in life
and in death advantage." This Geneva Version was that used
in Scotland for fifty years previous to the issue of the Authorised Version of 1611. The great house Bible which Bruce
called for on his deathbed, a book carefully treasured by his
descendants, is the Geneva Version, bearing the date 1561.
Principal Lee has gathered many interesting facts concerning
Scotland's preference for the Geneva Version. It appears that
Alexander Henderson read his text from it in preaching before
the General Assembly so late as 1639. Archibald Simpson gave
the very text which is found upon Bruce's tomb to his dying
brother, Patrick, and Master Patrick's answer was : " That was
a sibb sentence unto me before; my father spake it dieing."
(*Select Biographies,* vol. i. p. 102. See note in Hume Brown's
History of Scotland, vol. vi. pp. 108, 109.)

CHAPTER XIX

Seeing Visions and Dreaming Dreams

WHAT remains to be narrated concerning Robert Bruce in the present chapter may strike some minds as incredible: yet an honest biography must include the tale of the visions which were given to this saintly minister of the Scottish Church, and of that strain of the supernatural which characterised him in the later years of his life. What occurred in the instance of Alexander Peden we find also in that of Bruce: during his own lifetime a nimbus gathered about his brow; a number of curious miracles clustered around his name, as has frequently happened in the case of men of mystery, but especially in the case of leaders in the religious life. Readers of the biography of St. Francis, or of the marvellous history of St. Columba, will be able to compare the case of Bruce with many an episode out of the careers of these holy men. Indeed, in order to obtain parallels to his experience, it will not be necessary to go beyond several of his brethren, the Scottish confessors and martyrs. These miracles, if they have no other interest to-day, possess a real evidential value, in our endeavour to appreciate the career of Bruce.

Fleming, in a book called *The Fulfilling of Scripture,* wrote down many of these stories; strange haunting tales, which in the generation immediately succeeding lingered, as flowers linger still in what was once a carefully kept garden. At Larbert, it is told, the ministers of parishes and towns hard by, who were in sympathy with Bruce, loved to ride in his company when he went about the country. One stormy day Bruce rode with a companion towards the seat of their Presbytery. He had been in infirm health, and his friend was anxious lest he should suffer harm on account of the weather. To his astonishment he found that the rain which had drenched him through and through had not touched Bruce, save for a little dew upon the surface of his clothes. " Sir," cried he, " what is this? You seem hardly wet at all." The other expressed his surprise also, but, added he very quietly : " It seems my God has cast a cloak over me."[1]

Another story, whispered abroad at Larbert years after the death of Bruce, was that his body had been found undecayed when the grave was opened to bury a grandchild.[2] Surely they are sorely lacking in insight who fail to interpret stories like these. What are they but the shadows cast by this towering figure upon the page of history? It is true always, for instance, as the former legend teaches, that " God casts down His cloak " to cover His trusting children. It is also a fact, as is poetically told in the other lingering tradition, that the memory of the good man is blessed, while the name of the wicked shall perish. Not the body but the spirit and the influence of Robert Bruce are undecayed to the present hour, both in Larbert and throughout the Church.

John Livingstone in his *Memorable Characteristics,* and Robert Fleming in his *Fulfilling of Scripture,* relate several striking instances of the spiritual insight of their master, Bruce; and as both of these men had opportunity of knowing the facts, their evidence must be treated with great respect. The latter author says that he refrained from putting on record some of the stories which were in circulation, because they seemed incredible. His neglect is the loss of the Church. We could have measured better the character of our hero if we had obtained a full report of those whispered popular tales of his miraculous powers, just as one can calculate the height of a monument by means of the length of the shadow which it flings upon the ground. About the names of great popular leaders like Wallace or Washington precisely the same sort of legend has grown.

Wunderthätige Bilder sind nur schlechte Gemälde.

Bruce had a great natural sagacity, and the possession of

[1] Wodrow's *Bruce,* p. 149.   [2] *Ibid.,* p. 150.

that gift accounts in part for his shrewd words, and for actions which overawed simpler minds. The case of a man visiting at his Larbert house who, in the face of the minister's entreaty, persisted on leaving late at night despite the great rain and the swollen river, is typical. Master Robert was so anxious, that at length he declared he feared there was something amiss, and in the morning the body of the man was found in the river.

Then we trace in many an anecdote evidence of a keen spiritual discernment, as of one who was close to his God, and who therefore could read well the hearts of men. Coming to visit a dying person at Larbert one day, as he entered the sick-room, he marked intuitively the working of God's grace in the soul of the sufferer. " I perceive," said he, " that my Master has been here before me, and has done the work, so that there is little need for me." It was found that the case was even so, and that the dying man was in a frame of gracious trust.[1]

No less quick to detect unreal profession was the spirit of one so profoundly attuned to the will of God. A hundred years after his death there was lingering still in Larbert a credible story of a communion season at which Bruce presided. On rising to address the assembled partakers he continued gazing in silence. At length with much concern he broke out : " There is some person at this table guilty of a sin unrepented of; for my Master has shut my mouth, and I can say nothing till he remove. In the Lord's name I charge him to withdraw from this Holy Table." Having thus spoken he sat down, and amid breathless silence a man rose up from the communion table and left the church. Whereupon the minister resumed the service, and proceeded with much power. Afterwards it was discovered that this terrible " fencing of the table " had been justified, and that a most unworthy person had been induced to with-draw.[2] How revealing the incident is, both with regard to the manner of that time and with regard to Bruce himself, quick to detect any unwholesome presence, and as quick to respond to the presence of God.

On another occasion John Spottiswood, who had been at one

[1] Wodrow's *Bruce*, p. 149.   [2] *Ibid.*, p. 147.

time a zealous minister, but who had accepted a bishopric and
"sunk to the rear and the slaves," paid a visit to Bruce in
Kinnaird.

Bishop Spottiswood was essentially what the Scottish people
call a "Moderate." He could not understand how anyone
should suffer and go into banishment for trifles like those
points upon which the sturdy Bruce took his stand. Spottiswood was an unimaginative man, without any strong convictions, except perhaps to be dutiful to his King. The attention
paid by him to Master Robert in calling to inquire for his
health was kindly meant, but the old minister could not forget
that this man had sold his Church for a mitre. He was by no
means cordial to his guest, and he would not give him his
title when he spoke. At length the other said: "Sir, do you
not know me, and who I am?" The flame at last blazed up.
"I know you," he sternly returned, "to be a traitor to God
and to the Church of Scotland. I have nothing to do with you.
Begone, when you please."[1]

As an intercessor Master Robert had great power with God.
"Divers persons that were distracted, and some who were past
all hope of recovery in the falling sickness, were brought to
him, and after prayers by him in their behalf they were fully
recovered."[2] For every Christian knows that the effectual
fervent prayer of the righteous man availeth much.

There is a gift, however, quite distinct from any which has
been described, that of prediction. John Knox and John
Welsh were declared to be possessed of it, and Robert Bruce
is a third in whose utterances this power is traced. These men,
it is pointed out, had so deep an insight into the working of
God with His Church, they had so highly developed a spiritual
sense, that they could foretell events.

What of this? In Bruce's case it may have been only the
exercise of that shrewdness, allied with rare spiritual insight,

[1] Wodrow's *Bruce*, p. 152. David Dickson, the Melvilles, and
John Welsh adopted the same practice, declining to bestow titles.
See Young's *Life of Welsh*, p. 192; Cald., vol. vii. p. 539.
[2] Fleming, *Fulfilling of Scripture*, vol. i. p. 367.

which was certainly his possession. Michael Bruce, a minister in Ireland, who was a grandnephew of Master Robert, was credited with something of the same power.

One may compare Bruce advantageously with Alexander Peden, " the prophet." They had many points in common. Sons both of Scottish lairds, they were for conscience' sake alike homeless and landless throughout the most part of their careers. Both of them narrowly escaped the knife and the bullet, because they were true confessors of Christ. But the characteristic which marks them both out from the herd of men is this overawing supernatural gift of prediction. What more can the honest, sympathetic reader of these two men's lives say but this (which Peden's most sympathetic modern critic says of him) : " The secret of the Lord is with them that fear Him, and He will show them His covenant?"[1]

Some of these predictions are announcements of an impending judgment. Such is the instance of John Watt, deacon-convener of Edinburgh, who was shot dead on the Burgh Muir, April 1601. This man had been denouncing Bruce, and threatening him for the " 17th of December." Bruce, conscious of his own rectitude in the affair of the riot, warned the deacon-convener that a judgment would befall him for the wrong he did him.[2] When, four years afterwards, he met his untimely end, it was whispered abroad that Bruce's word had come to pass.

Tales like these were told of all the prominent Reformers. Another class of anecdote in the case of Bruce, and probably the most instructive of all, is that which shows how he was led to a decision in critical hours, or comforted or warned by a dream of the night. It is told of Samuel Rutherford that his very dreams were of his Lord. Master Robert Bruce was in like manner a dreamer of dreams. On one occasion he received a mysterious message of warning, when the Assembly was about to do a high-handed thing, at the perpetration of which his soul rebelled. The year was 1588, and a minister,

[1] Smellie, *Men of the Covenant*, p. 465, 1960 edition.
[2] Cald., vi. p. 104.

Gibson, of Pencaitland, was tried for bold utterances, when the Assembly determined to suspend him. As Moderator, Bruce would have to carry out the sentence. But the night before he was warned in a dream not to take a part, a voice saying in Latin: " Take no part in the condemnation of God's servant." In consequence of this he refused to take any responsibility for this act of the Assembly.

During the ordeal of his solitary antagonism to the royal will, Bruce had great support on account of these inward manifestations of the approval of God. Sometimes by a verse of Scripture, sometimes by a vision, sometimes by a strong premonition, he was comforted. As with St. Paul, who in Jerusalem or in Ephesus heard voices of the night, by which he was guided; so here. On one occasion Bruce was threatened to be deprived not only of living but of life itself. He was much depressed, and, having to ride into Stirling, he was filled all the way with forebodings. But it pleased the Lord to grant him that night a comfortable vision on his bed. Recommending himself to the mercy of his God, he dropped asleep. In his dreams he saw clearly how tremendous the difficulties were, but he also perceived that he must face them or die. At the last he resolved to hazard all in obedience to his God, and he felt a strong impulse to cry, " In and through Michael, the captain of the Lord's host, I shall prevail. O Michael! O Michael! Who is like the strong God?" The Lord had sent His angel to take charge of His servant, inasmuch as he was obedient. On awaking, Bruce wrote the dream down, and felt by it greatly consoled.[1]

Bruce told young John Livingstone, in the year 1627, that he had had the following vision in the night. He saw in his dream a great roll or book with black covers, flying in the air, and many black fowls flying around it. But whenever the book touched any of them they fell down dead. A voice, distinct as Livingstone's own, said in his ear, " This is the ire of God upon the ministry of Scotland." The black fowls were of course the black-coated ministers, and Bruce in his dream fell

[1] Cald., vi. p. 275.

to weeping and praying to God that he might be kept faithful, and might not be one of those who were smitten down. When he awoke his pillow was wet with his tears. The dream is quite in the style of John Bunyan or of St. John the Divine.[1]

It is well, indeed, when young men see visions; it is even better that old men should continue still to the end dreaming dreams. No persecutions could quench the ardour of this servant of God. In his infirmity he was much confined to his house; many people visited him, rather to obtain strengthening than with any idea of bringing it. One visitor asked him how matters stood between him and God, in his condition of frailty and decay. "When I was a young man," said he, "I was diligent, and lived by faith in the Son of God; but now I am old and not able to serve Him so much; yet He condescends to feed me with lumps of experience."[2]

There is one never-to-be-forgotten incident in connection with the Larbert ministry, vouched for on more hands than one. Hard by the old church was a chamber in which the minister spent his time between sermons. One day when many strangers, noblemen and gentlemen, besides the usual congregation, were present in Church, they wondered why the minister delayed to come forth from his vestry for the second diet of worship. The time was overdue, and as some of them had far to ride after sermon they called the beadle, and bade him go softly to the little ante-room, where Bruce rested, and request him in their name that he should return to worship as soon as possible, for they had far to ride. The foolish beadle, says Master John Livingstone, who relates the incident, understood not that the preacher was dealing with God. He was ignorant of prayer, as was the case with many in the land, so late rescued from Popery. He listened, he knocked softly, but the minister did not hear his knock, being absorbed in his intercessions for the people, and in prayers on their behalf,

---

[1] *Select Biographies*, i. p. 306.
[2] The word used by Bruce was the old word "sense," "lumps of sense," *i.e.* more than a taste, a satisfying portion of gracious experience.

that God should grant him a message. The beadle overheard some of Bruce's petitions, and returning to them that sent him, informed them that there was some One in the room with the minister; that he had heard Master Bruce many times say with great emphasis that he could not go alone to the church, and that he must have the Other with him, but that the Other answered him never a word. The invisible mysterious Friend, with whom Bruce spoke, did, however, in the end come out along with him, for the story goes on to tell that he issued after a little while from his chamber, and was singularly assisted, the service which ensued being remarkably useful to many people.[1]

So it came to pass that, through the practice of prayer and by the cultivation of his inner life, Master Robert Bruce overcame. Men feared or they sought his intercessions, as they had feared or had sought those of John Knox. They who overheard his supplications were filled with awe as they listened, somewhat as the disciples were overawed when they heard the Master Himself praying upon the Mount or in the Garden.

There is a chamber high up in the tower of the modern Church of Larbert—a church which stands nigh to the spot where Bruce prayed and preached, and where his dust lies buried. In this little chamber Robert Murray M'Cheyne held his Young Men's Bible Class—M'Cheyne who put on record in his Diary his debt to Robert Bruce, and the stimulus which he derived from the inheritance of the Reformer's prayers. The intercessions of these two sainted servants of God are to this day before the Throne : and they are the goodliest heritage of the Scottish Church; for so long as she has within her borders children like Robert Bruce and Robert M'Cheyne, who believe in the practice of prayer, she shall be still the Arm of the Lord.

[1] *Select Biographies*, i. p. 307; Fleming, *Fulfilling of Scripture*, i. p. 377.

CHAPTER XX

Thirty Sermons of Bruce recently Discovered

THE discovery of this MS., containing thirty sermons of Bruce, fully reported, must lead to a rekindling of the hope that ere long the lost narrative of Bruce's " Religious History," written by himself in his old age, may be produced. It is very probable that letters and other papers bearing upon the story of Master Robert Bruce are at present in the custody of people who do not know their value.

The present volume is very neatly written, having few errors or blots, so that it must have been the work of a skilful scribe, who took the sermons down verbatim " as they were received from the preacher's mouth." The handwriting is that quaint mediæval script which was soon to pass out of use, the texts at the top of each sermon being actually written in a more modern and to us more legible hand, for the scribe was so accomplished as to be the master of both styles. These texts are always from the Geneva version, though in the body of the sermon our author takes leave to quote in the homely Scots, which he also uses freely in his preaching, especially in the more emotional passages. It should be added that the volume is strongly bound in panelled calf, a style of binding which is certainly coeval with the writing, both being over three hundred years old.

This volume extends to 340 pages of closely-written matter, 43 lines to a page,[1] and at the end there are 28 pages of verses,

---

[1] Its possessor, the Rev. John Sturrock, has most generously placed the MS. at my disposal. In referring to it, I state the page not in the footnotes but in text of my chapter, so as to avoid confusion. As the leaves of the MS., and not the pages, are numbered, a [2] is affixed to the numeral when the second page of the leaf is quoted from.

of the type of the *Gude and Godlie Balladis,* evidently introduced in order to fill up the blank pages. These thirty sermons
are unquestionably by Bruce, and were preached in St. Giles
Church somewhere between the years 1592 and 1596. As his
name nowhere appears in the MS., there being no title-page
and very little that is personal throughout, it will be necessary
first to indicate the proof that these are genuine sermons of
Master Robert.

The thirty sermons are all preached from texts of Heb. xi.,
" The Honour Roll of Faith," and the first sermon opens with
a reference to previous sermons upon earlier chapters of the
same epistle. Hebrews was a favourite book of this preacher,
and he refers at so early a date as 1589, in the second sermon
upon the Sacraments,[1] to his preaching on Heb. vi. 6; as,
indeed, he was engaged in expounding the passage of Heb. xii.
14, 15, on 6th June 1591, in the presence of the king, when
he broke out in solemn warning to his Majesty with regard to
the prevalent lawlessness.[2] A sermon upon Heb. xii. 1, " The
great Cloud of Witnesses," printed at the end of Wodrow's
volume of *Bruce's Sermons,* is in reality the thirty-first discourse of the set in our MS. volume, forming an exact sequel
to the last of our series on Heb. xi., and having many allusions
in its course to the preceding exposition of chapter xi. Especially the preacher of this sermon upon Heb. xii. 1, recapitu-
lates the final paragraphs of the thirtieth sermon of our MS.
upon the uses of affliction and the cross. There are also several
phrases repeated from the closing pages of the MS., so that the
reader of the MS. cannot doubt that the sermon on the Cloud
of Witnesses is part of the same series. Now this particular
sermon on the Cloud of Witnesses, under the title, *The Christian Race,* was first printed in Glasgow in 1740, with the name
of Master Robert Bruce on its title-page; so that we have in it
strong evidence that the thirty sermons are by the same
preacher. On broader grounds of evidence every reader of the
present volume of thirty sermons is shut up to the conclusion
that they are by none else than Master Robert Bruce. No other

[1] Wodrow's *Bruce's Sermons,* p. 52.   [2] Cald., v. p. 129.

man in Scotland, in the end of the sixteenth century, could
have attained these majestic, passionate periods, with their rush
of eloquence as of a stream in spate, with their homely language that reaches the heart, with their sustained appeal to the
conscience, and their large human sympathy. There is a note
of command, and a constant sense of authority, which are in
character. "I have ever a regard to my warrant," says the
preacher.

And students of Bruce's earlier volumes will readily detect,
as they read these "Thirty Sermons," many a mannerism of
phrase or turn of expression which reveals the minister of St.
Giles. The usual opening formula of address, "Brethren, well-
beloved in Christ Jesus," and the doxology at the close of each
of these sermons are alike peculiar to Bruce. The latter is as
follows: "The Lord grant it for the righteous merits of Christ,
to whom with the Father and the Holy Ghost be all honour,
praise, and glory, for now and ever—Amen."[1] We recognise
in the MS. many expressions that are very characteristic of
Bruce, like, "Out of question," with the meaning "beyond
question"; "No doubt," for "doubtless"; "Come on, then,"
as he warms to his subject; the constant use of "therefore" to
clinch his argument. We have "Tak' heed to this," as, probably with finger uplifted, he drives home his lesson. God is
the "Living God," Christ is "The Maister." The natural man
is spoken of as "flesh and blude." There is a quaint old-world
humour, and a tendency to quote colloquial or proverbial say-
ings. For instance, when the preacher is driving home the
lesson that death may claim the young as readily as the aged,
and that we are uncertain at what hour it may please the
living God to *chap* on us, he adds, "It is said in your proverb,
As soon comes the lamb's skin to the market as the old
sheep's" (p. 91). "Lichtly won, lichtly tint," is Bruce's
form of the proverb which is better known as "Easy cam,
easy gang."

The homely words of the vernacular delight us in these
pages, as they did in Bruce's communion discourses. "*Spunks*

[1] See page 53 of this book.

of grace" is here, and the "*Hail* Christ," and the preacher wishes to *ding* the word into the ears of them that listen. Can any reader translate the following gem? In speaking of Joseph's obeisance to his father, Bruce expresses himself thus: "He falls down a-grouf and halsis his Father, and that with his bonat aff." We are here commanded, as formerly, to bid our affections good-night (p. 78).[1] Once more we encounter terms like "Preposterous affection for persons," "errors and stammerings." There is traceable the same delight to indulge in an occasional phrase borrowed from the law. "Spuilzie," in the sense "to spoil" or "rob," is the commonest of these; and we come upon words like "effeir," and "heritable infeftment." England is referred to as the neighbouring country; and the warnings to beware of Spain and the "Paipe," help us appreciably in assigning a date to these thirty sermons.

Indeed, the political allusions and the descriptions of the social condition of Scotland are among the strongest evidences that this book is the workmanship of Master Robert himself. Here is the well-known style of turning to each estate severally with warning or encouraging appeals. On at least one occasion James VI was present in his gallery the while Bruce preached from the text, "All these died in faith." He has been pleading for the extirpation of the contrary religion, "for it is a foul and horrible thing that they who are enemies to Jesus Christ should be suffered so long in a Christian country." His wrath is due to the too tender treatment dealt in high quarters towards Papists, who are really under sentence. The following dramatic passage finds a place in the peroration of the minister (pp. 59, 60):—

"Therefore," he cries, turning to the King, "once put to your hand and let me see your Majesty as instant in that cause as I have seen you sometimes in other things, and that ye, my lords, be as instant in it as I have seen you in other things. . . . Would to God this exhortation had force both in speaker and hearer, that, since ye must once die and your life goes on, and

[1] See p. 81 of this book. Affections = lusts in the usage of Bruce.

ye know not how soon He will *chap* upon you;[1] ye that are in
high callings may disburden yourselves of the sins of your
office and of your persons, that you may have His discharge
in your consciences, that all your sins are forgiven, and so in
death ye shall have life. The Lord of His mercy grant that I
(if it please Him) may see yet in my time before I die, some
order taken with these confusions, which, out of question, Sir,
sooner than ye believe, will totter your chair, (the throne)
except order be had. Therefore not only for the settling of the
throne of Jesus Christ, but even for the settling of your throne
also, and for the weal of your subjects, let this be done. That
once our mouths may be opened to glorify God in you, and to
crave blessings to you and to your spouse both, and that at the
hands of Jesus Christ."

No one who has made a study of the style of Bruce can
question, for a moment, the source of that passage. The " Sir,"
in addressing his king, is quite characteristic. The piece is but
one of many, wherein the preacher of these thirty sermons
gives faithful exhortation to the king, on account of his slack-
ness in administration. Nor did he forget his duty with reference to his Majesty personally. Here is a sentence of exhortation worthy to be graven upon every heart : " Think I to overcome a kingdom out of me that am not a king within me, or
to be a victor over other men that has not made a conquest of
myself."

There is a curious expression found once or twice in those
MS. pages, that contains a convincing token of their origin.
In a solemn discourse upon trouble of conscience, the preacher
declares : " When the Lord wakens thy conscience there is
never a sin but it shall start in thy memory, and bring such
a horror with it, that of all pains it is the greatest. Yea, *the
burning of the carcase in a hot lead* is nothing to the trouble
of conscience " (p. 6). At once there comes to the recollection
that passage in Melville's *Diary*, where Bruce's talk is given
concerning his own agony of conscience.[2] The other place in

---

[1] Chap=knock. The expression is very usual in these pages.
[2] See pp. 24-26 of this book.

our MS. where an exactly similar comparison is made, will be found at page 71, where the preacher refers to the struggle between loyalty to the king and to conscience. He had no doubt which ought to be preferred.

" The love of God and the holy fear of His Majesty should be predominant in thy heart. Suppose thou have to do with a king or an emperor, let not the love and fear of the king prevail, but lift up thine eyes to the majesty of God; and rather offend the king a thousand times than offend God once; rather cast off thy son, thy wife, and thy children, than fall in the offence of God. Learn to prefer God to the king. . . . Let princes put thy body to the most exquisite pains that can be, thou would'st think all the pains of the earth, *even if it were to be cast into a hot lead,* a quiet estate in comparison with the torments of the soul."

It may be now taken for a thing established without question, that these thirty sermons, recently discovered, are from the lips of Master Robert Bruce.

While the evidence proves conclusively that the sermons belong to the last decade of the sixteenth century, it is more difficult to assign to them an exact date. In all probability many of them were delivered by Bruce on more occasions than one. Some have references to the Sacrament of the Supper, having had their origin in a communion season (pp. 13, 13[2]), and the second and third sermons were delivered on successive evenings (p. 12[2]). Bruce preached on week-days as well as on Sundays, and some of these sermons would be spoken at the week-evening diet, though most of them are regular Sunday discourses, and in one peroration reference is made to " the whole things that we have been speaking these many *Sundays* bygone " (p. 50[2]). That some of the sermons were preached as late as the year 1596, is proved by the sustained and passionate argument of pp. 122, 123, which is the same as that of Bruce's Apology, given in Calderwood, in defence of the minister's flight. The text is : " If they persecute you in one city, flee to another," and with the cleverness of a trained advocate, Bruce pleads on the theme : " One may flee in heart and mind from the flock, while he sticks close to his living. If he find not fault with the tyrant and oppressor, or with the corruption of doctrine, he is guilty of this flight. If he show not up the sins of the people in their own colours, he is guilty of this filthy flight." Bruce's conclusion, from the example of Moses (Ex. v. 15), is identical with his conclusion in the Apology: "It is leisum[1] to depart, and to reserve ourselves for a better time" (p. 123[2]).

It will be necessary in this chapter to give some idea of the scope and teaching of these thirty sermons. The manner of their production by the pen of some devoted reporter necessarily interferes with their form. They are sometimes "rudely set out in homely terms," though there are many passages of great strength and eloquence. It is an advantage that they are given verbatim. We hear Bruce labouring at the repetition and simplifying of his argument, in order to reach his audience. We are also able to learn that, although necessarily those paragraphs which had a political savour were the special ones quoted by the historians, such as Spottiswood and Calderwood, the actual space given by Bruce to these topics was very small. His great and absorbing subjects are God and the soul of man; sin and salvation. He preaches incessantly concerning "that great jewel, a trew and lively faith," "incredulity, that foster of the devil," "the bruisit and the broken heart," "the slauchter of the affections," "the piercing eye of a living God," and "the Cross of Christ."

Truly, never did the Scottish Church find a more self-sacrificing defender than this minister of St. Giles. Her interest is foremost always in his heart. Moses' choice is applauded, because he prefers that estate which man, naturally, would have counted the worst. "He makes a choice of that poor estate of the Kirk of God; of that estate which was accompanied with ignominie, contempt, and poverty" (p. 114[2]). Everywhere in Scripture the preacher can extract warnings and guidance for the Kirk. Noah and his family, safely hidden in the ark, were the visible Kirk; Israel in the wilderness,

[1] Cald., v. p. 572. Leisum = permissible.

what were they but the Kirk of their time? And, in the esteem of Bruce, Scotland is the most favoured corner of the Kirk of God. He warns the people not to neglect the sacraments; and he teaches, "Only they that are in the Kirk are safe" (p. 148).

What a congregation thronged the floor and the galleries of St. Giles to hear these eloquent sermons! Each class of worshippers is singled out and exhorted. The king in his gallery; the judges, that they do justly; the "advocates at the barr," who are told, "There should not a speech proceed from you but as remembering on the life to come" (p. 156[2]); the great lords, who are reminded of the claims of both "kirk and commonweal." The young are appealed to, and the old. In a time when children were forgotten at Church, Bruce does not forget the little ones, whom he describes as a "gift of the living God" (p. 93[2]). Among his audience are the grave scholar and the university student: "Ye," says Bruce, turning to them,—"ye that like to confer (compare) the Greek, the Hebrew, and the Latin in studying Scripture" (p. 97).

The preacher is exceedingly sensitive as to the burden of his calling. "These admonitions," says he at the close of a searching appeal, "flow from me of mind to edify them, and to deliver me from their blood." "Come ye here to sleep," he cries; "come ye here for ostentation and show, as the most part of you do!" (p. 140). "I speak nothing," he said on another occasion—"I speak nothing of a malicious heart, but of love." "In respect that necessity is so urgent, I have admonished, and I will admonish again; and if I knew the particular, in respect it is a public particular, I could well reprove it publicly" (p. 146[2]). And here are words that remind us of Bruce's great master, Knox: "Saving the prince, whom I reverence always in God, I stand in awe of the faces of no men, but I dare reprove them. I regard not their feud nor their favour in the matter of my commission" (p. 146[2]).

The great secret of Bruce's power in the pulpit is the note of reality and urgency which is ever present in his words. The

world at hand has ceased to have any fascination for him, because two other worlds have opened out before his view: hell
beneath his feet, but also heaven and hope overhead. Conscience and the remorse of the soul goad him on always. And
to him hell consists chiefly in a conscience unappeased. As he
discourses on the heart-shaking theme he falls to prayer:—

"Lord, of Thy mercy, touch us! It is impossible that words
can persuade, except He of His mercy touch us, that ye and
I and every one of us may remead our conscience for the sins
wherein we have offended Him, and in time prevent that everlasting revelation and discovery. . . . For hell stands in these
two points chiefly: in an everlasting presence of sin, and in an
everlasting feeling of the wrath of God. These two ye shall
find perpetually, except in time ye remead your conscience
and incall for mercy. For whosoever incalls upon the name of
the Lord shall be saved."

What he has himself learnt to practise, he entreats all men
to seek likewise—the grace of inward recollection and daily
prayer:—

"If it were but once in the day, lift up your hearts to crave
eyes of God that ye may see heaven, that ye may see hell.
This ye should do every day, at least, before ye go to your
work or to your bed, and before you rise in the morning; this
should be your care to remember to crave of God, that ye may
get a sight of heaven, and a foretaste of it in your souls,
whereby they might be allured to go to it" (p. 136).

The man to whom this vision of the eternal world has been
granted, cannot be influenced any more by the common
motives which have their play with other men. He is an
enigma to observers, for they cannot apprehend the forces
which bear upon his soul. Men like St. Paul, Augustine, and
Bunyan, having a large measure of this revelation given them,
lived under the power of the world to come. Master Robert
Bruce, too, belonged to that choice order of beings. Early in
his life he had looked upon the divine face, and the vision had
never faded away.

In reading rapidly over those yellow pages, one's ear is

struck by the constant recurrence of some musical refrain, that becomes fixed in the memory. Such are the passages at page 59[2], "Life is ever going on," and at page 64[2], "God is a God to me." The former passage immediately precedes that addressed to the King, already quoted:—

"Last of all, remember that this life is a voyage, whereby ye are led unto death. For so soon as we enter in this world we make our progress to the end. So this life is a voyage, and not such a voyage as pilgrims have. For they may go on their journey and stay in some place for a day or a year, as they please. But from the time we enter in this life there is no rest for us, but *continually going on*, and every hour leads us to our death. So, when I look to the course of this life, I can compare it to no other thing but to a boat that has both wind and weather, that goes close before the wind. Let the boatman be eating, drinking, sleeping, or doing what ye please, the boat goes ever on to the port. So it fareth with the course of this life; do what we will, sleep we or wake we, our life is ever going on."

"Whosoever has God to be a God to him, do him injury who please, prince or people, God will revenge it. As on the other side, may I count God to be mine, and may I say in my heart and conscience that *God is a God to me*; for it is but a general seal to know that God is good, if I know not that He is a God to me. So if thou in thy heart mayest say and be assured that ' God is a God to me '; mayest thou say this; then I tell thee, the heart that may heartily say it, that heart has set the whole felicity of it on God only,—that heart makes God to be the armour of it, to be the storehouse out of which it will seek provision. It converses perpetually with God, and depends ever upon His providence; it counts the presence of God in bondage to be liberty; in poverty it counts the presence of God to be riches; in sickness it counts the presence of God to be health. Now he that may say, God is a God to me,' if he have to do with help, will not run to man, but to God, and will depend upon the help of God."

Bruce's restraint is remarkable. This is no John Bunyan to

"unlock his heart" before the people. He is a reserved Scottish aristocrat. He will not name the miscreant lords, if a more impersonal warning may suffice. "Were it not that I delight not to express names, I could design them" (p. 130). He tells nothing about himself. Surely never was any preacher so sternly self-repressive. Why does he not disclose something more of his French student life than a curt reference (on p. 61[2]) to the French Capuchins, whose superstitions he had seen? How comes it that there is never a word here about witchcraft? Bruce was at one time on a commission composed of two lawyers, two burgesses, and two ministers, " to discover wizards and witches, and examine them under torture."[1] It is an astonishing and indubitable fact, and we can only believe that he would exert his influence in the interest of a more humane treatment of those miserable beings. It remains that one searches the pages of Bruce in vain for any allusion to the unhappy victims of this persecution. He was absorbed in other questions, and the trend of his own mind was towards doubt and scepticism rather than towards superstition.

We could have welcomed allusions to the manners and customs of his age. We have only generalities. Scotland was once a land the most happy and favoured, now it is " a miserable country," kirk and commonweal being alike in danger. Now it has come to this pass, " that men doubt if there be a devil " (p. 162[2]). The preacher believes that the end of the world is near, because ignorance and infidelity are so great. We obtain a glimpse of the dumb, driven population; of criminals who escape justice; of a system of law which has failed to defend the people or to punish offences. The arm of the Church is impotent, and excommunication, once a real menace, is ineffectual :—

" We have but few excommunicates but are exceedingly well entertained, and their ward is no ward, but a further liberty; their punishment no punishment, but a further impunity; and their fear is nothing but a plain mockery. It is a shame to the

---

[1] *Register of Privy Council*, vol. iv. p. 680; p. lxiv.

country, to the King, and his council. I admonish you, my lord, as one of the special councillors, to put to your hand to this, that these men may conform to the religion of this country, or then let them be banished; not that I hate their persons, but I seek to win them. What noble or great man abhors these men? But they hawk and hunt, eat and drink with them as if they were not at the horne of Jesus Christ?"

The preacher sternly denounces " this whole country, partly mocking the word, partly mocking the ministers, partly mocking the judgment of God." Churches must be planted in various neglected parishes. Traders and merchants are warned against trafficking with the idolatrous country, Spain. Popery is a ceaseless menace. Bruce's plain words in expounding the story of Rahab show that he was well aware of the coarse, lewd life of certain dwellers in the city; his ear has caught the refrain of their "vain and baudrie songs." The following remarkable passage discloses the devoted minister's views upon pastoral visitation; and no doubt embodies also his practice, when, descending from the pulpit and putting off the black gown of his office, he went about in quest of the sick and fallen :—

" They are counted blessed by the mouth of the Spirit of God that visit the sick in their great disease; that come to comfort them that are visited by the living God. And there is an express command given to us out of the mouth of the Master so to do. And in the 25th Matt. it is told you in plain terms that the negligence of this duty in not visiting them who are visited by the hand of God, whether in body or in mind, shall be laid to their charge at that day, and it shall be said, ' I was sick and ye visited me not.' The sick ones would be visited, both with our word and with our person, and suppose ye have not the word of comfort presented in your mouth, yet excuse not your away biding, by the want of that word. For a sick man craves not many words. Their disease may not suffer long harangues; and, therefore, if thyself want the word of comfort, go to seek it in the sick man's mouth. For commonly the word of comfort in their mouths at that time is most ripe. And suppose you have no language, think that thy presence may do them good.

" For among many temptations that occupy the heart of the diseased, this is not one of the least. Syne that in respect of their diseases they cannot be able to serve in the world as they were wont to do, they think that they are casten off of all men, and none regards them. Therefore when their friends visit them, and refresh them sometimes by their sight, then they see that God has a care of them in making their friends to visit them. Therefore whenever any of your friends, or any of the members of Jesus Christ, are visited either in soul or body, if your leisure serve, go and visit them and comfort them with your presence " (pp. 89^2, 90).

In his old age, of course, Bruce claimed the privilege of his years, and gave the world a narrative of his soul's life. There is one place in these thirty sermons when he seems to tear away the veil of his reserve. Speaking of the efficacy of the Precious Blood, he says: " But when He finds the blood of Christ to have washen the soul and sanctified the heart, then He looks to the blood of Jesus Christ and in Him beholds thee, so that the justice of Christ compears for thee, the holiness of Christ compears for thee, *of the which two I am sure in this life by faith in Jesus Christ.*"

And in every page of the Sermons one must detect in the background a subjective allusion, and a personal application of the teaching, such as are inseparable from true proclamation of the Christian message. When may a man disobey the magistrate? he asks at page 111^2, and his answer, " When conscience and the Word of God are violated," was soon to find its best illustration in his own sufferings. He is discussing duty to men and to God, and starts the question, " What if the two are not compatible?" (p. 114). His answer is not doubtful. " Leave the duty you owe to men, and do the duty that you owe to God. . . . For so far as I can see, and so far as by the sight of things experience has taught me (yea, and I will ye read over the histories), ye will never find but he that studieth to please a man with the displeasure and offence of the Living God, God raises up that same man to displease him to the heart and to be a burriour[1] to him " (p. 114).

In speaking of the call of Abraham, he lingers upon it, describing it as a " calling," till we are reminded of that other " calling " (as Bruce was wont to describe his own experience), which took place in the new loft chamber of Airth Castle. " Then thank God for your calling; mark and perceive when it pleases the Lord to call you to the knowledge and insight of your sins in His mercy. Note the time, and ye shall see that the calling of God found you neither holy nor just, but of all creatures most abominable " (p. 40).

In like manner, it is impossible to miss the personal note in a passage like the following on the choice of Moses :—

" It pleased the Lord to send His servant to the school, and to a very hard school, even to banishment, in the which He holds him so long that He scours off all that courtly behaviour off him. He pulls off him all those old clothes that he had put on at court, and He rubs off all the manners that might have hindered the execution of his calling." He adds that Moses found that the court and his conscience could not agree, a form of words reminding us of the explanation given by Bruce of his own choice of a sphere for his ministry.[2]

This preacher is revealed in the Thirty MS. Sermons as a great scholar and theologian. While it will scarcely be expected that a man of the temperament of Robert Bruce can put forth his learning as some might, for display, there was in the Epistle to the Hebrews more scope for the production of such a gift than in the volumes of published sermons. There are evidences here that Bruce had an acquaintance with the archæology of Palestine, and *Josephus* has to be added to the list of his books already given :[3] " The famous historiographer, Joseph." Yet amid all his learning he is all the while a man of one book, and his Geneva Bible, " the great house Bible," or his Hebrew Bible, or his copy of the Septuagint, is far more

---

[1] Burriour = executioner.   [2] See p. 40 of this book.
[3] See p. 79 of this book.

to him than either Tertullian or Augustine. " I see," are his words in one place, " there is no true history in the world but these of the Bible. For the Bible, as it sets down the good properties of great men, so it conceals not their faults. The Holy Spirit is the true historiographer, and the Bible the only true history " (p. 153).

In Bruce is to be met one of the true, heaven-born interpreters of history, forasmuch as into his hands the key has been put which unlocks this door, and which admits to the possession of God's secret in His dealing with successive generations of the children of men. Faith is the key, and Bruce's testimony is, " When I was young I lived by faith." From his youth to his old age he was an example of them that overcome by faith in Christ. And as he expounds to us in these eloquent pages, the successive examples of " true and lively faith," those who fought and overcame, instinctively the reader who understands Bruce will feel the desire to take pen in hand and add yet another name to the roll of honour : " By faith, too, Robert Bruce of weake was made strong, waxed valiant in battell, turned to flight the armies of the aliants . . . whom the world was not worthy of : he wandered in wildernesses and mountains, and dennes and caues of the earth; and through faith obtained good report."[1]

The scholarship of Bruce is exhibited in our volume in so happy a fashion that it is necessary to make some longer allusion to this aspect of his teaching than hitherto was possible. That noble gift of the Scottish Renaissance, an accurate scholarship, is associated in our thought with men like George Buchanan and Andrew Melville, " those twins of learning " of whom every patriot is justly proud. Of the school which these masters founded Robert Bruce was an apt pupil. His knowledge of the sacred tongues was acquired at St. Andrews from the Melvilles, and it serves him well in his ministry. He can discuss the vowel-points of Hebrew; he knows both the Septuagint and the Latin Vulgate, or " Vulgar Interpreter," as he

---

[1] Heb. xi. 34, 38. I quote the striking Geneva Version which Bruce employed.

styles it. In expounding Hebrews xi. 21, and replying to the view of the Papists that Jacob worshipped his staff-head, as it were adoring a crucifix, Bruce is most effective. In the eagerness of his argument he actually lets slip a Greek word ἐπι, "which means 'toward' or 'fornent.'" We are delighted to find him in his treatment of Psalm lxxviii. 49, "Evil angels," anticipate the rendering of our modern revisers, "angels of evil": or to hearken while he considers the view that Rahab might be a "taverner" by trade. "The Hebrew word may tolerate another signification; they that have any entry in that language will know." But for himself he will have none of that interpretation. On Rahab's telling a lie to save Joshua's scouts, Bruce raises the question, "Was it right?" And he answers, as became a true Protestant: "No! and God will not allow of it. God is true, and this agrees not with God. And he rewards her not for that lie, not for that fault and infirmity, but for her faithful service."

The same balance of judgment directs his treatment of the method of turning history into allegory. Smaller men have come to grief by permitting themselves to allegorise, till the soul of man has rebelled at the device. "Suppose," says Bruce, "allegories be kittle, for myself I take no great delight in them; yet, where the ground is certain in the book of God, there is great profit and instruction in them." Consequently he allows himself to turn the story of Rahab and the fall of Jericho into a striking allegory (p. 145²).

Three hundred years ago certain points of textual criticism vexed this preacher, but the teaching of Andrew Melville sufficed to guide him. "Always supposing there be some difference in a word, there is no difference at all in the sentence and meaning." "When the meaning is preserved it becomes us not too curiously to dispute nor insist upon syllables and words. It is true that the Septuagintis (these Interpreters) have those words as the Apostle sets them down." "Whenever the Greek goes from the Hebrew in sense and meaning, or the Latin from the Greek (I mean from the original) in sense and meaning, in that case cast both Latin and Greek aside, and have recourse to the right meaning of the Spirit of God as it is set down in the original " (p. 96²).

In the theology of Bruce there is a slight departure at one point from that system which is identified with the Evangelical Church. It is always at the point where first a man encounters God that he retains the strongest convictions; and his teaching, if he teach other men, will turn around his own personal experiences. The centre of Bruce's theology is the conscience, and not the affections. In preaching, " renounce your affections," Bruce employs the last word in an archaic sense, meaning " lusts." But in our sense of the word " affections," *i.e.* the " feelings," Bruce does not make his appeal so much to them as to the more austere side of man's nature, the conviction of sinfulness. Conscience is our most awful judge. " For it is certain that the conscience shall be awakened, and the judgment of your conscience shall go before the judgment of God; so that no man shall be condemned, but he whom his own conscience first damneth, nor no man be justified but he whom his own conscience first justifieth " (p. 59).

The sting of conscience and the sense of sin urge on this preacher to proclaim salvation by faith in Christ, and he would drive men home to God under a sense of fear : " There is no way to heaven," he says, in sombre tones, " but hard by the gates of hell; no way to joy but by pain." And, in consonance with this doctrine, he preaches renunciation with the power of a St. Francis. There are a hundred places like the following, which could be quoted : —

" Therefore, rather than lose your soul, lose your affections. Yea, suppose thou should'st enter into the kingdom of heaven crooked, blind, and lamed of all thy outward senses, as the Master says, rather lose all than lose thy soul " (p. 54).

" Then, take heed! This is the first, out of question, and the last lesson, to learn to renounce yourself, and to take up your cross and follow Jesus Christ." " For it is better to come in the kingdom of heaven naked than to be clad with that curse which must drown thee for ever and ever." " Remember of

that promise which Jesus Christ makes in all the four evan-
gelists, that they shall not be that will quit anything for His
sake, but He shall recompense them, not only in the world to
come, but in this same world."

Indeed, the preacher admits that the lesson is hard to practise, but he has no novel suggestion, nor any recourse, or
prescription, save prayer.

" I know not any other way to practise it than I have told.
Therefore, cast you to resolve, and cast you to be instant in
prayer."

In keeping with this doctrine, and flowing out of it, is
Bruce's teaching upon good works, which he roots, not in the
heart, but in the conscience. In the following passage his
view is disclosed : —

" These deeds and good works are given thee in this life to
be a gadge and sure pledge that the perfect justice of Jesus
Christ pertains to thee. If we had not this pledge and gadge,
that the perfect justice of Jesus Christ appertains to us, it is
not possible that the conscience of any man could believe in
Jesus Christ, that His perfect justice was allowed to him. If
I began not to do well in myself, and wrought not according
to the Lord's command in my calling, my conscience could
never be persuaded of a remission, and of the free imputation
of the perfect justice of Jesus Christ. For, in continual evil-
doing, the conscience has a continual fear and vexation, and
must flee from God as from the enemy, and so the conscience
cannot keep faith, and without faith we cannot be sure of the
remission, nor of the imputation. . . . So to keep faith in me,
and to be a pledge of the perfect justice, this imperfect justice
is given me. When I do an ill turn, the conscience being
troubled, I dare not believe. No, there is not such a thing as
ever I can have resource to look to God for Christ's sake, until
the time I obtain some peace in my conscience. I am not
justified by the works that proceed from me, but by the works
which proceed from Jesus Christ, my Saviour, of the which I
am sure by a lively faith " (pp. 161[2], 162).

Here is another extract which we recognise as embodying the

essence of Bruce's doctrine, the closing text being that great epitaph of the preacher's grave in Larbert:—

"No marvel that a good cause makes a good and blessed death. For a good cause makes a good conscience, and he that dies with a good conscience dies well. So beware of the gnawing of an evil conscience. Eschew the torments of an evil conscience, and purge your conscience of everything wherewith it is defiled, and ye shall die well. So men should take heed to their quarrel, and have regard to their cause, that they cast not their life in danger for every light cause. But ere you put your life in hazard look what conscience you may have, in case you be slain. Look what report ye may have of God in case ye succumb. And if you find a good warrant in your conscience, whether ye die or live, ye die and live in God; but if you have no calling nor warrant in your conscience, I would wish no man to enterprise such a quarrel. But of all quarrels in the earth that bring blessings upon body and soul, and put us at ease here and at ease hereafter, is the quarrel of Jesus Christ. When a man offers himself to stand in the defence of the quarrel of Christ Jesus, and offers to hazard his body and life, there is a blessed quarrel. For there is no question, if we had experience how sweet Christ were, we would count (as the Apostle says, Philip. i. 21) Christ in death and life to be more to us than advantage" (p. 19).

Our last quotation from the Thirty Sermons is a strange one. Whatever gift of prediction Bruce may have possessed in regard to public questions, or even concerning other people, he can have had no premonition in the days of his Edinburgh ministry as to the place or the circumstances of his own burial, or he would hardly have spoken thus:—

"You will not find a man who dieth in the faith of Jesus Christ that will be curious of his burial, but he will be curious to send his soul to heaven, to recommend it in the hands of Jesus Christ. He will not take heed to outward pomps, in what place of the Kirk he will lie. No, commonly there is never a man who desires to *lie in the Kirk and to be placed nearest the pulpit*, but he who came never into the Kirk" (p. 104).

Forty years after the utterance of these words, Bruce's own dust was laid in exactly such a shrine as he describes with so great contempt. And he died, recommending his soul into the hands of Jesus Christ, and recommending also that Redeemer in faith upon whom he had lived.

While the present author has honestly tried to place the chief contents of these Thirty Sermons before modern readers, he is aware that it is impossible to convey by extracts the aroma of the ancient book. He can but declare the delight which it has given him to become acquainted with the sermons, and to introduce them to others. What has it been but (to borrow a simile from Horace) the unsealing of some cask of aged Falernian wine, with the brand upon it of the consul in whose reign it was stored away? Better; this has been like Mary's breaking of a box of spikenard, when " the house was filled with the odour of the ointment."

Finally, the hope is cherished that the present volume may serve some good purpose: by placing before our age the character of one of Scotland's forgotten heroes; by leading some to search for themselves in those fascinating neglected originals where Bruce's story is portrayed.

APPENDIX

As these sheets were passing through the press it was permitted me to see and examine personally Bruce's famous Bible, almost the only remaining item of his personal belongings. The book is in excellent preservation. A page, Gen. ii., etc., which had dropped out, has been carefully copied and replaced, the copyist cleverly imitating the form of print. The title-pages of New Testament and Old Testament are nearly identical, but the date on the Old Testament title-page is 1562, while that on the New Testament title-page is 1561.

On the fly-leaf there are entries of the birth of certain descendants of Bruce; but the most interesting study in this Old Bible is that of the marks opposite certain favourite passages, which if not by the Reformer himself, are by some kindred spirit, as anyone who notes the place of their occurrence will be convinced. The cross which appears against Rom. viii. 28, at " all things worke together for the best," is typical. Another mark can be detected at Rom. ix. 2. The passage on Gethsemane, Luke xxii. 40-43, is marked, with its significant phrasing of verse 31, " Satan hath desired to have you that he may wynow you as wheat "; and texts like Matt. xvi. 25, " Whosoever will save his life shall lose it," and that of Col. iii. 5, on mortification. Finally, I note the appropriateness to Bruce's case of a text like that marked out at 1 Cor. x. 13, " There hath no tentation taken you but such as appertaineth to man; and God is faithful." It is probable that these and the like marginal markings are from the hand of Robert Bruce.

BIBLIOGRAPHICAL NOTE

Calderwood's *History of the Kirk*, Row's *History*, James Melville's *Diary, Select Biographies* and the *Life of Robert Blair* are all quoted from the Wodrow Society editions published in the 1840's.

Spottiswood's History is cited from the one vol. edition of 1668.

M'Crie's *Andrew Melville* has been referred to in the edition of 1899.

The *Booke of the Universall Kirk* is quoted from Peterkin's edition, 1839.

The fragments of Robert Bruce's own narrative are found partly in the pages of Calderwood, partly in the publications of the Bannatyne Club.

Of the earlier works on Bruce the most notable is the volume published in 1843 from the MSS. of Robert Wodrow (1679-1734), consisting of *Collections for a Life of Bruce*, together with seventeen of his sermons. That Dr. William Cunningham could edit this volume at the height of the Disruption controversy illustrates his opinion of Bruce's worth.

The best known of Bruce's works, his five *Sermons on the Sacrament* were first published in 1590, reprinted 1617 (London, with eleven other sermons of Bruce), 1901 (edited by John Laidlaw) and 1958 (edited and retranslated by T. F. Torrance under the title *The Mystery of the Lord's Supper*).

This present book, first published in 1907, is the only serious life of Robert Bruce that has ever been written. A MS. volume containing thirty of Bruce's unpublished sermons was rediscovered while this biography was being written and these are described in Ch. XX.

INDEX

Paper-Backs

THE LIFE OF ROBERT MURRAY M'CHEYNE
ANDREW BONAR. 192 pp. 2/6

"This is one of the best and most profitable volumes ever published. Every minister should read it often."—C. H. Spurgeon.

LETTERS OF JOHN NEWTON
192 pp. 2/6

Although John Newton, the one-time slave-trader, became a prominent preacher, there is no doubt that his most useful and lasting work was achieved through his letters. This selection from his correspondence provides a mine of instruction and guidance for all.

*A SUMMARY OF CHRISTIAN DOCTRINE
LOUIS BERKHOF. 192 pp. 3/-

Here is an extremely useful and handy "miniature systematic theology" designed to meet the needs of the many who desire a reliable guide book on Christian doctrine. Ideal for Bible classes and Church bookstalls.

THE RICH MAN AND LAZARUS
BROWNLOW NORTH. 128 pp. 2/6

In the last great religious awakening which occurred in Britain just over a hundred years ago, there was no figure who drew more attention than Brownlow North. These chapters were originally preached to multitudes in the open air in the 1859 revival.
Ideal as a gift for non-Christian friends.

THE LIFE OF ROBERT BRUCE (1558-1632)
D. C. MACNICOL. 192 pp. 2/6

Evangelist, Expositor, Theologian, Leader, Robert Bruce, the successor of John Knox, was the foremost preacher of his time. This twentieth-century biography makes the seventeenth century live for modern readers.

FIVE CHRISTIAN LEADERS
J. C. RYLE. 192 pp. 2/6

"I believe firmly that, excepting Luther and his Continental contemporaries and our own martyred Reformers, the world has seen no such men since the days of the apostles."—J. C. Ryle.
Short biographies of Grimshaw, Rowlands, Berridge, Romaine and Venn.

FIVE ENGLISH REFORMERS
J. C. RYLE. 160 pp. 2/6

The purpose of this book is to remind men what our leading English Reformers did and taught, and what they suffered at the hands of the Church of Rome.

* An American edition of this title is available, and therefore this British edition is not for sale in the U.S.A. or Canada.

Geneva Series of Commentaries

"In order to be able to expound the Scriptures, and as an aid to your pulpit studies, you will need to be familiar with the commentators: a glorious army, let me tell you, whose acquaintance will be your delight and profit. . . ."—C. H. Spurgeon, from *Commenting and Commentaries*.

OLD TESTAMENT:

NEW TESTAMENT:

* *American editions of these titles are available, and therefore this British edition is not for sale in the U.S.A. or Canada.*

Other Titles

American editions of these titles are available, and therefore this British edition is not for sale in the U.S.A. or Canada.